THIRD EDITION

ESSAYS

that will get you into

Business School

Adrienne Dowhan, Chris Dowhan, and Dan Kaufman

BARRON'S

All inquiries should be addressed to:
Barron's Educational Series, Inc.
250 Wireless Boulevard
Hauppauge, New York 11788
www.barronseduc.com

Library of Congress Catalog Card No. 2009017335

ISBN-13: 978-0-7641-4228-4
ISBN-10: 0-7641-4228-3

Library of Congress Cataloging-in-Publication Data
Dowhan, Adrienne.
  Essays that will get you into business school / Adrienne Dowhan,
Chris Dowhan, Daniel Kaufman. — 3rd ed.
        p.   cm.
  Includes bibliographical references and index.
  Rev. ed. of: Essays that will get you into business school / by Daniel Kaufman,
Chris Dowhan, Adrienne Dowhan. c2003.
   ISBN-13: 978-0-7641-4228-4 (alk. paper)
   ISBN-10: 0-7641-4228-3 (alk. paper)
   1. Business schools—United States—Admission. 2. College applications—
United States. 3. Essay—Authorship. 4. Exposition (Rhetoric).   I. Dowhan, Chris.
II. Kaufman, Daniel, 1968–   III. Kaufman, Daniel, 1968– Essays that will get you
into business school.   IV. Title.
HF1131. B77   2009
658.0071'173—dc22   2009017335

Printed in the United States of America
9 8 7 6 5 4 3 2 1

Contents

PART ONE
Writing the Essay 1

PART TWO
The Essays   47

Acknowledgments

The authors of this book are all part of an Internet-based company called IvyEssays. Since its creation in 1996, IvyEssays' goal has been to help students gain admission to leading colleges and graduate schools by providing a variety of resources such as examples of previously successful essays and professional editing services. We are extremely happy to be working with Barron's on this book series.

We owe our sincere thanks to two groups of people. First, there are all of the students who have permitted us to publish their admissions essays so that they might help illuminate the way for future rounds of hopeful applicants. Second, there is the team of IvyEssays contributors made up of past and present admissions officers and professional writers who together have logged over fifty years of admissions experience. This series would not have been possible without the assistance of those listed below:

Joanna Henderson was the Director of Graduate Admissions responsible for MBA programs at Babson for four years and the Dean of Admissions at Colby-Sawyer College for five. She is currently the Director of the New England Admissions Office at Marietta College in Ohio and is an advisor/consultant for Stanley Kaplan Educational Center. She is the author of *ZINGERS! Creating Achievements from Ordinary Experiences*, published in 1988.

Miriam Ruth Albert is currently an Assistant Professor of Legal and Ethical Studies at Fordham University Schools of Business. She was a Legal Methods Professor and Associate Director of Admissions at Widener University School of Law where she counseled prospective applicants and evaluated over 400 applications. She also taught an LSAT preparation course for Stanley Kaplan Educational Center.

Amy Engle worked at the Hofstra University School of Law for more than seven years and served there as the Assistant Dean for Admissions.

Helen LaFave is currently an independent consultant who counsels prospective students through all stages of the admissions process. She has also served as Senior Programs Officer and Recruitment Program Officer at Columbia University where she helped numerous students through extensive graduate school application processes.

Amy Yerkes was an Instructor at the University of Maryland School of Medicine where she taught a course designed to increase the writing skills of prospective medical students for the Office of Minority Student Affairs. She has also taught at the University of Pennsylvania and is currently Assistant to the Dean at Johns Hopkins University School of Continuing Studies and a Lecturer at Western Maryland College.

Ellan Watts is the Dean of Admissions at the Columbia Dental School.

Thomas Vance Sturgeon has over eight years of experience in the admissions process as Associate Director of Admission at Duke University and Assistant Director of Admission at Guilford College. Mr. Sturgeon is currently the Director of Admissions and College Placement at the South Carolina School for Science and Mathematics. Today, Mr. Sturgeon is a widely published author and lecturer on the subject of college admissions. He has been quoted in *Money Magazine's Guide to Colleges* and published in the *Journal of College Admission*.

Marcy Whaley is the former Associate Director of Admissions at the California Institute of Technology and Assistant Dean of Admission at Illinois Institute of Technology. She has over a decade of experience in college admissions and is currently an independent admissions consultant and freelance technical writer.

Scott Anderson is currently Associate Director of Admissions at Cornell University. Mr. Anderson's past experience includes the position of Assistant Director of Admission at Vassar College, and he has been on the admissions staffs at the University of Vermont, St. Michael's College, and the University of Virginia.

Patricia M. Soares is an independent educational consultant for underprivileged youth with years of experience as an admissions officer. She has been the Assistant Director of Admissions at Connecticut College and an admissions officer at Rhode Island College.

IvyEssays was founded based on the belief that some people have far more access than others to the resources and information that improve one's odds of getting into the top schools. While admissions officers do their best to take these disparities into account, it is up to students to equip themselves for the application process to the best of their abilities. Our goal is to help level the admissions playing field by providing resources that might otherwise be available only to the more privileged. Good luck and good writing!

Introduction

- Your essays are the only part of the application process still within your control.

- Your essays allow you to distinguish your application from the others.

- This book provides you with examples of successful essays, inspiration for essay topics, and a comprehensive process for writing effective application essays.

How would you feel if getting into the business school of your choice had nothing to do with your grades, work experience, or test scores? Imagine for a moment that the admissions officer finds only your essays when she opens your file. She must base her decision solely on the ten or so pages you have crafted—a decision that will affect the rest of your life.

If this really occurred, would it make you elated or simply nervous? Would you feel like you were given an incredible opportunity? A second chance? Regardless of how you feel about the essays, try to think of them as being exactly that, a chance. Everything you have done up to now is complete—past tense. Even if you have impressive work experience, strong test scores, and a good undergraduate record, this is not the time to rest on your laurels. Your essays lie ahead—treat them like nothing else matters. As one admissions officer stated,

> *The essays are the only aspect of the application over which the applicant has total and complete control.*

According to admissions committees at top schools around the country, the essays play the crucial role of humanizing you. Think of your essays as representing the face of your application. Without them, your application is little more than a statistic—just another faceless person in a crowd. A member of our staff has said,

> *The admissions committee wants, above all, to see a real person. The essay is virtually the only tool that the applicants have to bring their files to life. Good essays make an applicant human, memorable, and "accept"able.*

An applicant with poorly written essays does not give admissions officers the opportunity to care. Use basic psychology. Make the admissions committee feel that they know you, and it will be harder for them to reject you. Make them know and like you, and they might accept you despite your weakness in other areas.

Additionally, the essays give you the opportunity to highlight strengths that would otherwise go unnoticed. An admissions committee member explained,

> *The essays give the applicants a chance to showcase their strengths beyond simply their scores. In other words, sure, they worked at a top consulting firm and scored well on the G.M.A.T. So did everyone else in this stack of hundreds. At some point we are going to ask, "What else?"*

Essays can demonstrate maturity, purpose, depth of character, an ability to think clearly and logically, a sense of humor, leadership ability, confidence, intelligence, attention to detail, and professionalism. Whatever your strengths, here is the one place where you can emphasize them. If you succeed in writing essays that demonstrate all of the above, you have probably also written your ticket into the school of your choice.

Understanding the importance of the essays is a necessary first step toward writing effective ones. However, that knowledge alone will not do you much good. In fact, if all it does is make you nervous, it can even hurt your efforts. So if all of this has you sweating, you can relax now. Taking the essays seriously is the first step. We are here to help you get through the rest.

What We Have Done

We have developed a powerful program to guide you through the process of writing effective essays. This book will arm you with the tools you will need and strategies that work. We will help you determine the content of your essays, get the words onto paper, and polish your work to perfection. Here is an overview of what you will find ahead:

1. **Preparation and Strategy:** Before you can begin writing, you need to devise a plan of attack. In Chapter 1, we help you understand what your essays need to accomplish by giving you a better understanding of your audience. (Who are the admissions officers and what do they really want?) In Chapter 2, we help you gather the materials you will need to write your essays. (What details from your past experience should you use and where?) Once these questions are answered, Chapter 3 will help you devise a strategy to convey information in a personable and compelling way.

2. **Writing:** In Chapter 4, your fingers will meet your keyboard as you begin writing your first drafts. We will help get you through even the worst case of writer's block. This chapter will introduce you to a number of different structures for presenting yourself and your ideas as succinctly as possible.

3. Editing: This step, introduced in Chapter 5, is crucial. We will show you how to take those first drafts and work them like pieces of clay. You will need to write and rewrite, think and write again, until your essays distinguish you from the other hundreds of applications the committee will receive.

4. Read Examples: Finally, one of the best ways to learn and get inspired is to read essays written by applicants who successfully gained entrance into the schools you wish to attend. Located in Part Two of this book are over fifty essays divided by question type. This section includes advice and tips for how best to tackle each one.

As you follow the steps presented in this book, keep focused on writing the best possible essays. Try to remember that for the moment, nothing is more crucial to your ultimate acceptance—and nothing is more under your control. With that in mind, let's get started.

A Note About Plagiarism

Throughout this book, we have emphasized the need for honest, personal application essays. To submit anything else to the schools where you are applying is not only stupid—it's illegal.

If you do borrow material from other sources, be sure to credit it properly. If you are not careful about this, you may hurt your chances of getting into a particular school. To purposely avoid giving credit where credit is due is to court disaster.

In Chapter 1, an admissions officer is quoted as saying, "After fifteen years of reading hundreds of essays a year, you develop an amazing ability to see straight through the bull." This is also true of detecting plagiarism. Admissions officers do read hundreds of essays every year. In doing so, they have developed a sense of whether or not the author of the essay is being honest. Although it may sound impossible, these admissions officers also tend to remember many of the essays that they read. If it is discovered that you have "borrowed" someone else's essay, you will undoubtedly be denied admission.

You owe it to yourself to be honest, forthright, and sincere.

PART ONE

Writing the Essay

CHAPTER 1

Assess Your Audience

- The goal of your essays is to convince the admissions committee to accept you.
- Above all else, admissions committees want INTERESTING essays.
- The committees look to your essays to distinguish you from the others.
- Your essays should provide evidence of solid writing and communication skills.

Straight from Admissions Committees:

- Tell stories—entertain us.
- Be yourself.
- Use details and examples.
- Utilize humor.
- Be personal and honest.

- Don't be dull or predictable.
- Do not use gimmicks.
- Do not make lists.
- Avoid sarcasm.
- Do not whine or make excuses.

When we write, we imagine an audience. Consciously or not, we write for that audience. If you picture the admissions committee as a group of dry, nitpicky academics or solemn, medieval executioners, your essays will become dry, nitpicky, or solemn themselves. If you were to make this mistake, you would slowly but surely whittle the humor, risk, wit, and creativity out of your essays—the very ingredients essential for your success.

In this chapter, we take some time to get to know the real individuals who will read and evaluate your essays: who they are, what they look for in an essay, and what they are tired of finding. Without a clear understanding of your audience and their expectations, preparatory work is less informed and purposeful than it could be. You risk writing a set of essays that may be technically fine, but ultimately underwhelming.

Who They Are: Understanding the Committee

The truth is that admissions committees—even at the toughest business schools—are simply groups of individuals, each with their own interests and opinions. Contrary to popular belief, they want to read essays that will gain its author admission. A member of our staff has said,

> *The vast majority of admission officers are "people persons." We shrink from using statistics in the admissions process and see those who rely on them as cold, calculating, and unconcerned with individuals. We are warm, friendly, helpful, eager to please, and anxious to keep a human face on this cumbersome process.*

Business school admissions committees come in many shapes and sizes. They can comprise as many as a dozen or more members including admissions staff, faculty members or advisors, and students. Instead, they could include no more than a handful of members consisting only of professional admissions staff. While the structure and composition of the committee differs at every business school, your application will follow a similar path at each.

Demystifying the Admissions Process: What You Can Expect

Have you ever tried to imagine what happens to your essay after you submit your application? For many applicants, this part of the process is a mystery, but it does not have to be.

First, your file (application, transcripts, test scores, recommendations, and essays) will be read in its entirety by at least one, and usually by two or three, members of the admissions committee. This means that your application will never be summarily dismissed based on any one factor such as your G.P.A. or G.M.A.T. scores. It also means that no matter how you scored—no matter how well or how badly—your essays will still receive some attention. An admissions officer stated,

> *I personally can remember times at Babson when everything else in the file was mediocre. However, because the essays were so good, we called the person in for an interview to get another look.*

Admissions officers spend anywhere from ten to forty minutes looking at a given set of essays. One officer explained,

> *Essays are a huge part of the business school application. They are VERY important, so most counselors spend a lot of time reading and evaluating them. We might read twenty sets in a day, including what we take home at night.*

Twenty sets translates into over 100 individual essays per day. This is why, when asked for their number one pet peeve, admissions officers answer, "Boring essays!" and "Essays that all sound the same!" When asked what their number one piece of advice for applicants is, they answer, "Put yourself into your essays, and make them interesting!"

Once an application has been given a first, quick read, it will go into one of three basic piles: accept, reject, and unsure. A committee member stated,

> *Usually, two kinds of files go through easily and aren't read by more than two people: the truly outstanding because the file is so brilliant and the truly outstanding because the file is so poor.*

If your application is in either the accept or reject categories, it will generally be read by one additional person for confirmation. If the application is rated acceptable, the second reader is usually the dean. If the second reader agrees with the first, the process is complete. All other applications—and this is usually upwards of 75 percent—fall into the unsure pile. That pile then gets subdivided into probably accept, probably reject, and unsure—and so on and so forth.

The longer your application remains in the unsure pile, the more similar your numbers and background will be to the others in the pile. When competition gets tough, your essays become virtually the only tool you have to make your background and experience come alive, distinguishing you from the rest of the homogenous crowd.

What Committees Look For: Eight Key Attributes

During that first, quick review of your file (transcripts, G.M.A.T. scores, application, recommendations, and essays), every admissions committee uses essentially the same questions:

Will this person succeed academically at this school?

Will he or she contribute and add diversity to the class?

How does this person compare with the other applicants?

When they read your essays specifically, the committee members look for much more than this. The eight items unanimously cited as "most important in a successful essay" by our admissions advisors follow.

You will be offered much advice in the upcoming pages. You must not lose sight of the ultimate goal of the essays: *you must convince the admissions committee that you belong at their business school.* Everything we tell you should be used as a means to this end. Step back from the details often to remind yourself of the big picture and to make sure that everything you write focuses on your goal.

1. Givens

No matter which specific question you are answering, you need to accomplish a few fundamental goals when you write. Admissions committees do not specifically look for these basics because they are expected and should be transparent in good writing. To make sure you have addressed these fundamentals, use the following checklist for each essay that you write:

Have I answered the question asked?

Have I made clear, precise, understandable points?

Is my writing natural, concise, and error free?

When you have finished an essay set, or all the essays required for one school, step back and take a look at them as a whole. Make sure that you have done all of the following in at least one of the essays:

Demonstrated your motivation

Targeted the school

Expressed at least one to three qualities, strengths, or attributes that make you stand out from the crowd

Presented at least one solid and succinct argument for why the committee should accept you

2. Writing/Communication Skills

The essays also serve to showcase your language abilities and writing skills. A member of our staff said,

> *Your essay doesn't need to peg you as a future author or scholar but as a future leader in management. That said, the ability to communicate ideas and to present them skillfully is essential to success in the business profession, and good writing stems from good overall communication skills.*

Again, admissions committees seek good writing skills—they expect them. A beautifully written set of essays alone will not get you admitted to business school, but a poorly written set could easily keep you out.

3. A Real Person

What the committee really seeks in the essays is simple. More than any specific background, characteristic, or skill, they want to see a person. Admissions staff are adamant about wanting to feel that they know the human being behind the numbers. One explained,

> *We are searching for some intangible quality in the application that no number could ever reveal. We hope to find it in the essay. Never squander the chance to tell us who you are in the essay. It helps us to reassure ourselves that the process is human and that what we do for a living matters to another human being.*

Knowing this, it might not surprise you to learn that the number one piece of advice from admissions officers and business students regarding the essays is almost always the same. Although they expressed it in many different ways (be honest, be sincere, be unique, be personal, and so on) the advice is always the same—be yourself! An admissions officer explained,

> *Business applicants get so caught up in wanting to seem like something: a leader, mature, or, God forbid, "businesslike," that they forget to be something. We never get to know them.*

4. A Personal Approach

The only way to let the admissions committee see you as an individual is to make your essays personal. When you do this, your essays will automatically be more interesting and engaging. They will help you to stand out from the hundreds of others the committee will be reviewing that week. One committee member said,

> *Personalize your essays as much as possible—generic essays are not only boring to read, they're a waste of time. They don't tell you anything about the applicant that helps you get to know that person better.*

Since this is such a crucial factor in all good essays, most of the essays included in the second section of this book use a personal approach. One, though, stands out from the rest in this regard. If you are unclear about what is meant by making your essay personal, read Essay 34. As you read, are you able to picture the writer? When you have finished, do you feel like you have gotten to know her? She accomplishes this by integrating personal experiences and using details to bring it all to life. The writer is straightforward and honest. However, she relates her points in a light, informal, and almost confidential tone, more as though she were talking to a good friend rather than writing for a group of evaluators. Taking the personal approach to this extreme can be risky. When done with the skill and confidence this writer possesses, though, an extremely memorable and captivating essay results.

5. Details, Details, Details

To make your essay personal, take your cue from the writer of Essay 34 and use plenty of details. An essay without details is like food without flavor. It might fill you up but who wants to eat it? Members of our staff have said,

Details provide the color, the spice, and the life of the essays.

Generality is the death of good writing.

Each and every point that you make needs to be backed up by specific instances, examples, and scenarios from your experience. These details make your story special, unique, and interesting. Look at the detail used by the writer of Essay 12, for example, in the second half of the essay entitled "Learning to Surf." She moved in "August 1992," lived in "Paris for 21 years," averaged "90 hours a week," started "Bright and early on a sunny Saturday afternoon" despite "pale skin and weak arms." This could have easily boiled down to, "I moved from another country to the United States. Since I was working long hours, I decided to learn how to surf." This shows the difference between a fun, interesting treatment of a story and a yawn-inducing account that could be attributed to any of a thousand different people.

Develop the good habit of backing up all your assertions and claims of success with detailed descriptions of results. Use actual numbers and statistics if you have them. Essayist 19, for example, asserts, "I was quite successful as a tutor." That statement standing alone would not convince anyone. It would probably seem like little more than an inflated (and pompous!) claim had the author not backed it up with the following: "One young man increased his Math S.A.T. by 150 points. Another student improved so dramatically in geometry, her test scores jumped from about 55 percent to over 90 percent, that her teacher kept her after class and asked if she was cheating."

Although it is true that the use of excessive detail can slow down the pace of a story, don't even think about limiting the scope of what you incorporate during the first phases of writing. Too much detail in your writing is a much less likely pitfall than the alternative. To begin, err on the side of too much information and you can trim it down later. This way you won't find yourself manufacturing detail to fit neatly into an essay you thought was complete, but that turned out to be less than engaging.

6. Something Different/Unique/Interesting/Funny

Being different is easy—after all, you are a unique person. Showing how you are different is harder, but this is what will make you stand out. In order to accomplish this, take calculated risks. An admissions committee member explained,

Business applicants should not be afraid to go out on a limb and be themselves—even when that means incorporating humor or being a little bit controversial. They are so often concerned with making the correct impression that they edit out anything that would help their essay stand out. They submit a "safe" essay that is, in reality, sterile, monotonous, and deadly boring.

If your background is off the beaten track, do not play it down. Given comparable experience and success, an unusual background gives you a distinct advantage. Essayist 39, for example, knows how to take advantage of his uniqueness. He makes it the subject of his essay by stating in the first paragraph, "Because I am one of the world's few Catholic, Egyptian Mississippians who went to an Ivy League School, the particular set of influences affecting my development has been distinctive." Do note, however, that the writer of this essay does not get lazy by relying on this distinctiveness alone to carry him through. He still makes the connection of why, exactly, this distinctiveness has made him a better, more qualified candidate and how it will allow him to contribute to the business school community.

Even if you do not have a markedly different background, you can still be creative and come up with an interesting slant on an ordinary life event. Essayist 3, for example, could have appeared as a very typical applicant with an investment banking background. Instead, he pointed out that he "chose a slightly different route from most accounting majors at Wharton" by not "joining one of the Big Six accounting firms after graduation." By doing this, he makes his otherwise standard background seem nonstandard and makes the reader want to know why this (suddenly unique) person chose a different path.

7. Honesty

This point should be upheld without exception. Nothing about the application process could be more simple, more straightforward, or more crucial. Be honest, forthright, and sincere. Admissions officers will not tolerate hype. Do not try to create a larger-than-life impression of yourself or, worse yet, of someone you think the committee would accept. You will be perceived as immature at best and as unethical at worst. Members of our staff have said,

If you think you know what we want and you're trying to write for that, forget about it. There is nothing more obvious, and more humiliating, than doing a bad job of being someone else. Just be yourself and let us do the deciding.

After fifteen years of reading hundreds of essays a year, you develop an amazing ability to see straight through the bull.

Some of the essayists in this volume go so far in being honest that they admit to weaknesses, mistakes, and other instances that could be seen as drawbacks, even when they are not specifically asked to do so. Essayist 34, for example, admits that she was, "Never much of a student," and indulged in the "occasional prima donna fit." Essayist 23 writes that, "Some friends are quick to label me a dork." However, being sincere does not mean that you have to admit to your every folly. Drawing attention to negatives is not a requirement of truthfulness—you can be honest and still be completely positive about yourself and your qualifications. Ultimately, it is a very personal decision. If you do call attention—in any way—to your drawbacks, be sure to get plenty of objective feedback. You should feel confident that you have addressed these weaknesses with finesse and have not weakened your stance.

8. A Story

Admissions officers also look for essays they can enjoy reading. Some have explained,

Make sure that your essay is readable. Don't make us work. Give your essay momentum—make sure the parts work together and move to a point, carrying the reader along.

Use a conversational style and easy-to-understand language to project a genuine, relaxed image.

Humor is a powerful tool, so use it wisely. Gimmicks are a big mistake, and a sarcastic or flippant tone will often offend. Real humor, inventiveness, and dry wit, though, are always in good taste.

You can utilize the above advice in three ways. First, write your entire essay in the form of a story. Second, use a story to introduce your subject. Third, use an informative, conversational, or humorous tone as though you were telling a story. Some admissions officers cautioned against including this advice. However, others so enjoyed receiving a good story essay that we decided to include it with a caveat. This approach can be effective but is best accomplished by candidates with proven writing abilities. No matter how good a writer you are, be sure to get feedback and advice from as many people as possible before submitting an essay of this type. Even if the story entertains, you still need to communicate your motivation, ability, and maturity.

Some essayists take the first (and most risky) approach by writing their entire essay as a story. Essay 20, for example, says all it needs to say in the context of pure action. The essayist literally offers no explanatory text (and none is needed!) anywhere in this description, which is very rare for this genre of writing. Even his last sentence, "Because I know that I'm my own toughest competitor, and I'll always have to run a little bit faster if I want to keep up," where he communicates his main point, is still within the context of the activity.

The more common method of integrating a story into an essay is to tell the story first. Then, step back into the role of narrator and explain why the story was presented and what lessons were learned. This is a safer approach and more broadly employed but still very effective. Essay 31, for example, presents a very touching account of an experience during a trip to a lesser-developed country. The author steps out of his story only in the last paragraph, summing up his failure and subsequent resolution in retrospect. This results in a very powerful and believable narration. Essayist 15, for another example, employs a similar method using a very different type of experience, a hockey game. He even breaks his story into titled segments, "The Lead-In," "The Situation," "The Test," and "The Decision," mirroring a sportslike use of the play-by-play to heighten the sense of action.

What They Are Tired of Finding

Not surprisingly, much of what admissions officers are tired of finding is simply the converse of what they hope to receive. In other words, do not try to be something you are not. Do not lie. Do not hand in a poorly written, ill-constructed document riddled with grammatical errors.

Admissions officers, however, cited a few pet peeves so frequently that they bear repeating. After all, they would not be pet peeves if people were not still doing them.

Don't Be Dull!

The "don't" named most often by business admissions staff was, "Don't be dull!" This pitfall is especially rampant among business applicants due to the stereotyped image of what business schools want. Applicants know that maturity, leadership abilities, quantitative skills, and strong business experience are all extremely important. Essays written to fit this image are dry, boring, impersonal, and generic. Remind yourself that other qualities such as humor, adaptability, and a humanistic bent are also valued. Write to show off your own unique qualities. A member of our staff explained,

> *Everyone knows that we look for mature students with solid business backgrounds. What they don't know is that we also value other qualities very highly. Do these students care about people? Have they volunteered or contributed to their communities in any way? How have they developed themselves as people outside of the business world? We want interesting, multidimensional people, not workaholic, money-hungry automatons.*

Other traps that contribute to a dull essay include recapitulating facts that can be found elsewhere in your file, giving excuses, and writing in a dry manner. To avoid the first trap, make sure that your essays contain more than just a prose listing of your accomplishments and work experience. A committee member explained,

> *Listings of anything are dull, no matter how impressive they might look to you at the time. Save them for the other parts of your application.*

Most applicants find the second trap harder to avoid—but it does not have to be. When you have a poor grade or test score that you would like to address, give an honest and sincere explanation for the lapse. However, do not offer excuses. A staff member stated,

> *If you want to explain about a bad grade or low score, that's okay. Too often, though, the excuses are lame, and the candidate comes across as whiny.*

To keep the committee from groaning (or snoring!) when you try to explain a blemish on your record, be concise. You will find several examples of the correct way to offer explanations in the "Miscellaneous" chapter of the essay section of this book.

Even when your subject matter is interesting and you have no lapses to worry about, you can still fall into the third trap. Do not undermine your topic by using a dry writing style. Two admissions officers emphasized,

> *Don't bore us! More often it is the monotonous style, and not the subject matter, that makes these essays dull.*

> *What do I hate? Large words used clumsily. Colorless adjectives and weak verbs. Long lists of activities and accomplishments.*

If you are not a natural writer, you should have someone—perhaps a professional—give you thorough feedback and advice.

Don't Be Gimmicky

If dull essays are bad, essays that rely on gimmicks are worse. The consensus among our admissions team is clear. "What might have been cute at the college level of admissions simply won't cut it at this level of competition." One team member explained,

> *Every season someone sends us poetry. Once I actually saw a whole essay done as a poem. It should never be done; it just doesn't work.*

Although creativity can be achieved without this kind of gimmick, a fine line exists that should never be crossed. Even a well-executed approach when it attempts to be too creative becomes risky. A staff member stated,

> *When the creative approach works, it always seems like a great idea. However, the tough part is that the admissions committee is made of many types of personalities, some formal and old school and some more modern. The odds of a new, creative approach appealing to all (or even to a majority) of these personalities is slim.*

Mind the Mechanics

You have no excuse for including typographical or grammatical errors in your essays. These types of errors are easy to correct and costly if they go uncorrected. One shocking but surprisingly common mistake is forgetting to replace the proper name of the school throughout the essay. Each year, Harvard receives essays beginning, "The reason I want to attend Stanford. . . ."

We have listed below a few other common mechanical errors as cited by our admissions team:

> *Keep the essays within reasonable length. Excessively long essays show a lack of consideration—we have thousands more like yours to read, and seeing a long one just makes us tired.*

> *Don't cram your essay onto the page with a tiny font. If I can't read it without a magnifying glass, I won't read it at all.*

> *Stay away from lots of S.A.T.-type big vocabulary words. It's obvious who wrote their essays with the thesaurus in hand.*

> *ACTUALLY ANSWER the question they ask. Many people just list off their accomplishments and never relate it to the theme of the question.*

> *Proofread! Have others proofread! Spell check! It's stunning how many people have careless, even really obvious typos in their statements. It makes the applicant look sloppy, uninterested, unintelligent.*

Get Feedback!

This has been mentioned several times already but it bears reiteration: It is imperative that you get feedback on your essays before submitting your final versions. For a variety of reasons, many of the "don'ts" listed above are hard to spot in your own writing. Find an honest, objective person to read the entire essay set for one school. As comforting as it might be, do not accept a simple, "They're great!" Ask the reader to look specifically for the "do's" and "don'ts" listed in this chapter. Ask that person to recount to you the main points you were trying to make. Have the reader describe the impression he received of your strengths and weaknesses. Approach the same individual a week after he read the essays and see what (if anything) has remained memorable. Finally, if that reader is not familiar with what a successful admissions essay looks like, have him or her read some of the samples from Part Two of this book to use as a guide in judging your work.

Lastly, do not rely on only one person's opinion, especially if you know the person well or disagree with the points that person has made. Even the most objective reader has his or her own set of biases and opinions, and no one person can accurately predict the reception your writing will have at the school to which you are applying.

One way to offset this potential risk is to make one of your evaluations a professional one. Receiving professional feedback assures that the advice you get on essay content is based on evidence of what admissions committees are looking for and that grammatical feedback is coming from people with solid editorial experience. The authors of this book, with help from admissions officers and experienced editors, created a website for this purpose. At Ivyessays.com, you can upload your essays and choose different levels of feedback depending on where you are in the writing process. If you are only in the rough draft phase of putting your thoughts together, you can submit your essays for *quick feedback.* You don't need to worry about the grammar or mechanics at this stage. Editors will focus on the content of your essay and will send you tips and advice on how to improve it. If you are further along in the process, you can submit your essays for a *full edit,* and editors will provide a full mechanical and grammatical review.

Prepare

- Make an inventory of your activities, skills, and accomplishments.
- Create a list of your qualities and examples that demonstrate them.
- Make note of your major influences and how they've shaped you.
- Use the chronological method to record all meaningful experiences.
- Identify your personal and professional goals.
- Write each essay question on a blank page and add all relevant topics that you've identified.

Now that you have a better understanding of your audience and some of their opinions about what makes an essay exceptionally good or bad, you may feel ready to begin writing. Before you do, stop for a moment and assess your situation. You should now have a sense of the type of essays you want to present to the admissions committee, but you do not have the tools and materials you need to begin. If you were a painter, for example, you would need more than paint and a good set of brushes—you would need a clear idea of exactly what you were going to paint. Similarly, creating an essay full of imagery and detail will require you to think carefully about your subject matter before you begin writing.

Knowing what you are writing about means much more than simply knowing what your topic will be. It means, first and foremost, that you know yourself. You cannot afford to have a fuzzy sense of your motivations, skills, accomplishments, and goals. These things need to be solidified in your own head before you can communicate them effectively to others. Second, it means that you have identified the specific points you wish to make in response to each different question. Third, it means that you have chosen concrete details to use in support of each of these points. You will have to answer between three and ten questions for each school. Each essay will require between one and three points to support your claim and between one and three examples to support each of your points. Therefore, you should begin by appreciating the volume of material required to do the job right.

In this chapter, we help you collect this material. We begin with the basics in "Start Your Engines." The brainstorming activities in this section are designed to help anyone having trouble getting started—from those who simply have not found a place to begin and need a bit of a push to those who are suffering from full-fledged, panic-induced writer's block. If you can already clearly articulate your reasons for going to business school, your major strengths and weaknesses, and your goals for the future, then you might want to skip this section and go straight to "Gather Your Material." Before you do though, realize that brainstorming can uncover excellent material for your essays that your typical thought process may not produce.

Everyone will be making similar general claims ("I am intelligent, different, and unique and you should accept me. . . ."). Therefore, you need to pay special attention to making your essay stand out by using vivid examples from your past experiences. If writing an essay is a battle for you, the battle is won with details. Gathering details is what "Gathering Your Material" is all about. The brainstorming exercises found here are intended to help you uncover the specific experiences and influences that have shaped who you are today. These details will provide unique, interesting, and colorful content for your essays.

Start Your Engines

This section is intended to help those who are struggling with a blank page. If getting started is your stumbling point, or if you just need some additional fodder to keep writing, this section will offer some solutions. The point of the exercises provided here is simply to open the channels and get your thoughts and words flowing. Anxiety encourages the censor in our minds that criticizes everything we write. This censor hampers good writing, spontaneity, and originality. If you listen to it, your writing will be stilted and stale.

For these exercises, put all "do's" and "don'ts" aside. Forget about the specific questions you have to answer. Do not think about what the school or the admissions committee wants. Do not compare yourself with your competitors. Do not worry about grammar or style, and especially do not worry about what anyone would think. Instead, focus on writing quickly, recording every thought you have the instant you have it. You can even throw these pages away when you are finished if that helps you free yourself from constraints. You will know that you are performing these exercises correctly if you are relaxing and having fun.

The Inventory

This exercise is designed to get your pen moving. The goal is simply to compile an inventory of your activities and accomplishments—school, sports, extracurricular activities, awards, work, and pastimes. You may have already made a similar list during the application process. If so, start with that list and try to add to it. This list will become fodder for topics to use when writing your essays. During this exercise you do not need to write down any qualities, skills, or feelings associated with the activities. For now it is more important to be completely comprehensive in the breadth of topics and items you include. For example, if you taught yourself chess or particularly enjoy occasional chess games with your uncle, you do not need to be in the chess club or have won a trophy to add it to the list. Think of how you spend your time each and every day, and include any items that seem significant to you. Spend no less than twenty minutes writing, and keep going for up to an hour if you can. If you run out of items quickly, don't worry—you will probably come up with more during the other exercises.

Stream of Consciousness

Take twenty minutes to answer the questions, Who are you? and What do you want? Start with whatever comes to mind first and write without pausing for the entire time. Do not limit yourself to any one area of your life such as your career. Just let yourself go, be honest, and have fun. You might be surprised by what kind of results can come from this type of free association.

Morning Pages

If you have the discipline to practice this technique for a week, you may end up doing it for the rest of your life. Keep paper and a pen at your bedside. Set your alarm clock to ring twenty minutes early. In the morning when you are still in bed and groggy with sleep, start writing. Write about anything that comes to mind, as fast as you can, and do not stop until you have filled a page or two.

Journal Writing

Keep a journal for a few weeks, especially if you are stuck and your brainstorming seems to be going nowhere. Record not what you do each day but your responses and thoughts to each day's experiences.

Top Tens

Write down your top ten favorites in the following areas: movies, books, plays, sports, paintings, historical eras, and famous people. Step back and look at the lists objectively. What do they say about you? Do you see a pattern, or do any particular passions present themselves? Lastly, have any of your favorites had a significant effect on your outlook, opinions, or direction?

Free-Flow Writing

Choose one word that seems to appear on many of your questions such as *influence, strengths, career, diversity,* or *goals,* and brainstorm around it. Set a timer for ten minutes and write without stopping. Write down everything you can think of that relates to the topic, including any single words that come to mind.

Gather Your Material

If the exercises in the last section have successfully stirred your thoughts and animated your pen, then it is time to impose more focus on your brainstorming. These next exercises help you do just that. They focus more on finding the specific points and details you will need to answer each of your questions. However, be sure to retain the open mind and creative attitude with which you approached the last exercises.

First, write down each question you have to answer for every school at the top of a sheet of paper—one question per page. As you work on the upcoming exercises, you will now have all of the questions fresh in your mind as well as a place to jot down items specifically related to each question. For example, as you use the Chronological Method below to uncover experiences throughout your life, you may come across a point or example that seems well suited to answering one of the questions. Make a note of the item on the page with that question, and then go right back to brainstorming. If you can apply one situation or experience to multiple questions, do so. At this stage of the writing process, more is better—we address the techniques of honing and culling in Chapter 3, "Strategize." The objective now is to accumulate multiple points for each question, including at least one concrete example to back up each of the points.

The Chronological Method

Start from childhood and record any and all special or pivotal experiences that you remember. Go from grade to grade and job to job, noting any significant lessons learned, achievements reached, painful moments endured, or obstacles overcome. Also, include your feelings about those occurrences as you remember them. If you are a visual person, drawing a timeline might help. Do not leave out any significant event.

Since so many questions ask about your past, this exercise will help you uncover material that you will likely use in several places. A few schools will ask you directly about your childhood and have you highlight a memory from your youth. Be cautioned in advance, though. For many other questions, delving too far into your past for your examples will detract from the strength of your points. Most business schools are more interested in what you have been doing since college, for example, than in what you accomplished, no matter how impressive, during high school.

A childhood example can be well used to demonstrate a long-standing passion or to emphasize how an aspect of your character is so ingrained that it has been with you since youth. Essayist 19 does this, for example, when explaining his passion for math by writing, "I can remember riding in a car for long distances as a child and continuously calculating average speeds and percentages of distances covered as we traveled." His next example then jumps to college where he, "Took upper division math classes such as Real Analysis and Game Theory (and placed near the top of the curve) though they were not required for my major." These are both good examples of the kind of material that can be uncovered using the chronological method.

Assess Your Accomplishments

Write down anything you are proud of doing, no matter how small or insignificant it might seem. Do not limit your achievements to your career. If you have overcome a difficult personal obstacle, be sure to list this too. If something is important to you, it speaks volumes about who you are and what makes you tick. Some accomplishments will be obvious, such as any achievement that received public accolade or acknowledgment. Others are less so. Many times, the most defining moments of our lives are those we are inclined to dismiss.

The most evident use of this material will be in answering the accomplishments question. These moments will be useful in many other places as well, so do not stop brainstorming after satisfying this question. Many accomplishments, for example, address ethical dilemmas or demonstrate your leadership skills. Instead, they may relate to an extracurricular activity that you can then highlight in answering, "What do you do for fun?"

The essays included in the second half of this book demonstrate a wide range of accomplishments, ranging from the obvious and impressive such as Essayist 9 who has competed in the Ironman Triathlon World Championships to the more accessible topic of learning to surf in Essay 12. The main thing, again, is not to worry about how big or small the accomplishment is in anyone else's eyes. Simply write about what is personally meaningful to you.

List Your Skills

Do a similar assessment of your skills. Do not limit yourself to your business-related skills such as quantitative or leadership abilities. Cast your net broadly. Begin by looking back at the last exercise, and list the skills that your accomplishments demonstrate. When you have a list of words (*perseverance, time management, focus*) start brainstorming about the actions you have taken that demonstrate these skills. Pretend that you are defending these skills in front of a panel of judges. Stop only when you have proven each point to the best of your ability.

Note that a fine and fuzzy line exists between skills and personality traits, and use it to your advantage. Almost any quality can be positioned as a skill or an ability if the right examples are used to demonstrate it. The hockey player who wrote Essay 13, for example, lists initiative/entrepreneurship, perseverance, and time management/breadth of experience to answer a question about his accomplishments. Each of these could be considered as a skill or simply a trait. However, because he does such a good job convincing us of these qualities—using one experience from work, one from his extracurricular involvement, and one from his college life—it does not really matter if they are skills or traits.

Analyze Personality Traits

Take advantage of the fuzzy distinction between skills and traits as noted above. If you are having trouble listing and defending your skills, shift the focus to your qualities and characteristics instead. Make a few columns on a sheet of paper. In the first one, list some adjectives you would use to describe yourself. In the next one, list the words your best friend would use. Use the other columns for other types of people—perhaps one for your boss and another for family members or coworkers. When you are done, see which words come up the most often. Then, group them together, and list the different situations in which you have exhibited these characteristics. How effectively can you illustrate or prove that you possess these qualities? How do these qualities reflect on your ability to succeed at business school?

An extremely wide range of qualities and characteristics can be used to your advantage in the essays. The writer of Essay 11, for example, sums up, "Challenging and creative state of mind, ability to learn fast, striving for professional excellence, team spirit and willingness to cooperate, strong self-management—these are my most contributing qualities." Many writers stress their humanistic side such as their integrity, as in Essay 40, and their dedication to public service, as in Essay 24.

Note Major Influences

You can refer back to your Top Ten lists for help to start this exercise. Did a particular person shape your values and views? Did a particular book or quote make you rethink your life? Relationships can be good material for an essay, particularly one that challenged you to look at people in a different way. Perhaps you had a wise and generous mentor from whom you learned a great deal. Have you had an experience that changed how you see the world or defines who you are?

What details of your life, special achievements, and pivotal events have helped shape you and influence your goals?

A wide range of questions on business school applications pertain to influence. The most popular types of these ask about your mentors. However, many also ask about general personal, familial, or childhood influences or about specific professional influences. Some admissions officers caution against using a parent as an influence, simply because it is done so often. However, many of the essayists featured here reference the strong influence their parents have had on them and do it well, such as Essayist 40. Others speak more generally of family influence, such as Essayists 38 and 39. Alternately, essayists who reference professional influences include 24, who writes about both a professor and a boss, and 25, who writes about his manager.

At this and every stage of brainstorming, do not hesitate to expand and modify lists that you created previously. If at this stage of the process you realize that a strong influence in your life was not in your original list, that doesn't mean it is any less important to you. Add it now. The subconscious mind has an interesting way of retrieving information like this, and the brainstorming process is meant to uncover as much of it as possible, in whatever way it surfaces.

Identify Your Goals

The first step of this exercise is to let loose and write down anything that comes to mind regarding your goals. What are your dreams? What did you want to be when you were a kid? If you could do or be anything right now, regardless of skill, money, or other restrictions, what would it be? Think as broadly as you wish, and do not limit yourself to professional goals. Will you have kids? What kind of house will you live in, and what kinds of friends will you have?

The second step is to begin honing in on some more specific or realistic goals. Given your current skills, education, and experience, where could you expect to be in twenty years? Where would you be ideally? How does having an M.B.A. affect these goals and outcomes? Think in terms of five-year increments, listing actual companies, positions, and salaries if possible. Where will you be five years from now? Ten? Fifteen? Be detailed and thorough in your assessment. When you think you are done, dig a little deeper. How will your goals affect others?

Some of the essayists in this book are extremely specific about their future goals. For instance, Essayist 1 lists actual companies and positions he could step into once he has received his degree, while Essayist 37 already knows that he wants to be a college professor. It is not necessary to know your future this definitively. Essayist 2, for example, whose short-term goal is to "Develop my general management skills," and long-term goal is to be "The C.E.O. of a corporation, possibly my own," is general without being ambivalent. Even essayists with currently undefined goals can show that they understand the options that will be open to them and grasp the possibilities and potentialities. It is perfectly acceptable to wait for the further knowledge that will be afforded through the M.B.A. program to make final decisions. Essayist 3 does just that. He sums up his stance in the last sentence with, "Although not all of my post-M.B.A. career plans are definite, I know that the Dartmouth College Amos Tuck School of Business will invariably play a definable and pivotal role in the rest of my life."

Again, do not forget to hone in on your personal goals as well. Some schools ask you about this particularly. The writer of Essay 33 discusses her goal of marriage and children. Essayist 37 places all of his goals—personal and professional—in the context of the larger aim of being a philanthropist. Positioning professional goals in the context of a larger life plan is the sign of a determined individual living a purposeful life.

Before You Move On . . .

Thoroughly knowing yourself and all of your goals can be difficult. Not all of your motivations, significant influences, defining experiences, or career goals—especially the long-term ones—are going to be completely clear to you at this point. However, if these exercises proved more than a little difficult for you, it could be a sign that you need to step back and reassess your decision to get an M.B.A. Vague and unformed motivations and plans might indicate either ambivalence or lack of knowledge and research. Before you go any further, reassess your decision to attend business school. Look more closely into what an M.B.A. will do for you and whether it will allow you to achieve what you truly want. After all, if you do not clearly know exactly why you want an M.B.A. and what you will do once you have one, how will you be able to convince an admissions committee to accept you?

On the other hand, if this chapter helped you, you should now have plenty of material—in fact, more than you need—to write successful and convincing essays. The next chapter, "Strategize," will help you understand how to present this material as a cohesive whole. It will help you leave the committee with a strong sense of who you are and a persuasive, targeted argument for why they should accept you.

CHAPTER 3

Strategize

- Identify the most critical personal and professional points that you want to make.
- Strategically incorporate these points into the available essay questions.
- Make sure your responses effectively answer the questions asked.
- If submitting the same essay to multiple schools, make sure to tailor it to each question and each school.

You should now have collected more than enough material to use in your compositions. It is time to decide which pieces of information should be used and where and how to arrange them best. If you skip this step and attempt to use everything you have collected without discrimination, the essays will lack the focus they need to convey something meaningful about you. Apply this advice not just to the individual essays you write but to your entire essay set and the impact it will make in its entirety. The whole in this case really is greater than the sum of its parts. You need, in other words, to put as much thought and consideration into the structure, balance, and impact of your essay set as you do into each of your separate essays.

This chapter represents the last step you will need to take before creating your first draft. The first section, "Choose Your Weapons," presents strategies for culling the information you have gathered to identify the most important points you need to make. The second section, "Plan Your Attack," presents ideas for arranging this information within the overall essay set for greatest impact. The last section, "Use Shortcuts—With Caution," helps you to save time by strategizing similar answers to questions asked at the different schools—but also points out the risk inherent in not doing this step well.

Choose Your Weapons

One of the biggest mistakes business school applicants make is cramming their essays full of every detail they have uncovered about themselves. Due to fear of leaving out something crucial, some applicants force laundry lists of accomplishments, honors, and significant experiences onto the readers, which (as we know from the first chapter) is one of their biggest pet peeves.

Considering the wealth of material available to you—from your skills and accomplishments to your family background, academic life, extracurricular interests, career development, and professional and personal goals—choosing what to use and highlight can be a difficult and frustrating step. The secret to knowing how to say a lot without saying too much is to learn how to focus. All the material you have gathered can be brought together to support just a few of the most important points you need to make. To help you identify these points, try the exercises below.

Develop Your Personal Points

Look back through all the material you gathered in the last chapter. Examine the attitudes, expectations, achievements, strengths, and weaknesses the exercises have uncovered. What stands out as unique, distinctive, or impressive about you or your life story? What are the most recurring nouns, verbs, and adjectives? If either too much or too little emerges, prompt yourself further. Ask yourself why you do the things you do, what motivates you, what gets you up early and makes you stay up late. Be completely honest. When you are through brainstorming, look at the qualities that came up most often and, more importantly, by which you most want to be defined. Create a list of three to five personal points—the points most crucial to communicate to the committee. Some examples could be integrity, strong international experience, commitment to the community, or time management skills.

Create a Career Profile

This is similar to the last exercise but focuses your attention on the professional sphere. Separate out the brainstorming material you have gathered that is specifically related to your career goals and past experience. Look at it objectively. What does it tell you about your professional interests and attitudes? What does it tell you about your motivation? What themes or points emerge repeatedly? Are these the qualities you wish to express? If you are not satisfied with the image you see, keep probing. How have you changed since you started your first job? What did you know about it then, and what have you learned about it since? What has prompted you to pursue it further or reinforced your certainty that this field is ideally suited for you?

Again, try to reduce the material down to between three and five points. These will be the themes that you need to build on throughout each essay set. Make it your goal to ensure that the reader finishes your essays with a very clear sense of these points.

Plan Your Attack

When you have finished deciding which personal and professional points to use, you need to put some thought into how best to incorporate the points using the different questions available to you. You can use your points as a theme running throughout most (if not all) of your essays, or you can decide to focus on a different point in each essay. In the end, how you do it does not matter as long as the essay set clearly communicates each of your points at some stage. In fact, you will probably end up with a combination of these approaches. Rely on your own best judgment, and use these methods to spur your thoughts.

The Categorical Method

Looking back to your personal points and career profile, think about the different categories representing the different aspects of your life. Your categories might include your career, academics, extracurricular activities, community and volunteer work, and family experiences. Into which categories do each of your points fall? Are they distributed evenly throughout, or do you favor one or two over the rest? Which of these areas take top priority in your life? Which commands most of your time?

When you have categorized your information into some broad areas, begin thinking about which questions can be used to convey each category. Picture your essay set as a jigsaw puzzle. Each essay provides a different piece of the puzzle and, when put together, forms a single image. For example, the Why M.B.A.? question can be used to focus on your career, the extracurricular question to talk about your hobbies, and a leadership question to talk about your community involvement.

Do not be afraid to be creative when it comes to fitting the different areas of your life into the framework of the questions as long as you answer the question asked. You might want to talk about your athletic achievements in the accomplishments question, for example. However, then surprise the committee members in the question about extracurriculars by focusing on your more recent exploration of print making.

For an example of an applicant who applied the categorical method to his essay set, compare Essays 29, 31, and 51, which were all written by the same person:

Essay 29: (*Extracurricular*) Focuses on his extracurriculars by describing a failure in a game of squash.

Essay 31: (*Ethical Dilemma*) Focuses on his career and ethics by describing a trip he took as part of his job to a factory in a lesser-developed country.

Essay 51: (*Miscellaneous*) Focuses on his academic strengths, highlighting his ability to contribute to the case study method.

Each essay is so targeted to a single area, experience, and argument, respectively, that it would be impossible to know that these were written by the same person without being told. When taken together, though, a well-rounded, multi-dimensional, and dynamic personality appears.

This approach can be good for a candidate with a broad range of skills and experience. The pitfall is that if you do not create a compelling picture overall, you may appear fragmented and unfocused—moving in too many directions at once. The next approach—using theme—takes exactly the opposite approach.

Think Theme

A very different way of planning a big-picture approach is to think in terms of developing and building the same theme throughout all or most of your essays. In other words, prove and support the personal and professional points you uncovered in the previous sections again and again using a different angle or set of experiences in each essay.

This approach is usually attempted only if an overriding quality or achievement in your life has become a major part of your identity—if you are, for example, a professional athlete or musician. Be aware that by using the theme approach, you will be assigning yourself a very specific identity. You will be known among the committee as the rower, or the violinist. This can work to your benefit by making you more identifiable and memorable. However, be sure that you would want to be associated with this identity.

An example of someone who uses a theme approach is the hockey player who wrote Essays 13 and 15. In the first of these, he focuses on his perseverance and time management skills by highlighting the dedication and time needed to participate and succeed at that level of the sport. In the second, he focuses on one particular athletic experience that highlights his integrity and leadership skills. Each essay enriches our appreciation of what we have learned in the other.

The pitfall inherent in this approach is appearing one-dimensional. The best way to avoid this is to choose a broad, multilayered theme. In other words, do not just focus on being an Olympic rower and leave it at that. Focus on the combination of qualities needed to become an athlete of that caliber. Explore your theme thoroughly, and do not expect the experience or accomplishment itself to convey everything on its own. Take a different angle or stress a different aspect of the quality or experience in each essay.

Another pitfall to avoid is redundancy. If you are going to talk about your trip to Nepal in answer to the accomplishments question, do not repeat the same story or make the same points to answer the contribution question. You will be wasting a valuable chance to add dimension and depth to your character.

A Combined Approach

A good plan of attack for any applicant is the combined approach. This approach takes the best aspects of the categorical method and combines them with thematic style by structuring the essay set as though it were itself an individual composition. A combined approach treats your first essay as an introduction by introducing all themes and making all major points. The middle essays support these themes by honing in on a different point, area, or aspect in each. The final essay (usually an open/optional essay) echoes the introduction by summarizing and reiterating all major points and themes. However, it goes one step further by adding a new insight of dimension.

An example of someone who has used the combined approach is the writer of Essays 4, 19, and 49:

Essay 4: (*Why M.B.A.?*) Introduces himself on a broad level, highlighting the personal points of his background, his goals in marketing, qualitative skills, team-player approach, and teaching/management ability.

Essay 19: (*Extracurricular*) Provides evidence for teaching and quantitative skill by focusing on his experience as a math tutor.

Essay 49: (*Open Sell*) Concludes by summarizing the strengths of his application, hitting on all major points and then developing further insight by mentioning his disability and reapplication.

Use Shortcuts—With Caution

You have probably already figured out that you can save yourself time and energy by tailoring answers to questions for one school to use for similar questions at different schools. If you are creative, you will be able to plug in many of your answers into some not-so-similar questions, too.

Consider, for example, the two situations used to answer a leadership question in Essay 17. The essayist could have easily applied the first experience of uncovering a miscalculation and deciding to work around the clock to amend it to answer an ethical dilemma question from another school. Her second example of managing a client engagement could have doubled as a response to an accomplishments question in a different set. Either one of these could also have been used to answer a question about teamwork. Also take the example of Essay 31 in response to an ethical dilemma question. Because the situation resulted in a negative experience, he could easily have opted to use this to answer the failure question instead.

As you can see, the possibilities for swapping data are endless. Lifting whole paragraphs and applying them to different questions is fine—as long as you do so seamlessly. Be absolutely sure that you have answered the question asked. When a school notices that you have simply swapped essays without even bothering to tailor it to the question at hand, it reflects poorly on your sincerity. This indicates to the committee members that this is not your first-choice school. Essay 9, while an exceptional essay in and of itself, is a good case of just such mistaken identity. Although the question asks about his distinctiveness and how it will enrich the learning environment, the essayist's answer was clearly written to answer questions about his influences. This is evident even from the first sentence, which begins, "Different people, events, and situations in my life have shaped who I am today and the distinct blend of these influences has made me the individual I am."

If you do want to swap data, the best places to tailor your answers are in the first and last paragraphs. To correct the problem with the above essay, for instance, the essayist need only focus the first paragraph around distinctiveness instead of influence and conclude in the final paragraph with how these experiences will help him to contribute. All the actual content in the middle could have remained untouched.

Before You Move On. . .

We have stressed in numerous places throughout this book the importance of proofing your essays and getting feedback. While most applicants are good about taking this step after writing individual essays, some forget to apply the same advice to their essay set as a whole. Before you send in your application, be sure to assess the impression your essays will make when taken together. Use the following checklist to be sure that you have addressed the large-scale problems that you can miss even after diligently proofing individual essays:

- Are the main points that I am trying to make evident?

- Do redundancies or apparent contradictions occur between essays?

- Do the essays present a cohesive, coherent image throughout, and does each essay contribute to the same image?

- Do the essays use a consistent voice and style throughout? Do the essays sound like the same person wrote them?

- Does the essay set support the impression made in the rest of the application?

- Does the essay set address red flag issues that appear throughout the rest of the application (for example, inconsistent academic performance, lack of community involvement, and so forth)?

CHAPTER 4

At Last, Write!

- Creating an outline is essential to achieving structure and focus in most types of essays.
- Effective leading sentences are critical to sparking interest and introducing themes.
- Smooth transition sentences are necessary in creating cohesive paragraphs.
- An effective close should be relevant to the essay as a whole and leave a lasting impression on the reader.
- Unusually short or long sentences can interrupt the flow of your essay and make it more difficult to read.
- After writing your first draft, take a break before attempting to revise it.

Now that you know what you want to say in each of your essays, it is time to start writing. Set a time limit of no more than one day for each essay. The longer your time frame, the more difficulty you will have writing your first draft. Do not allow yourself to sit around waiting for inspiration to strike. Some of the worst writing ever crafted has been done under the guise of inspiration.

Relieve some of the pressure of writing by reminding yourself that this is just the first draft. You will have plenty of time to perfect the essay later. For now, you just need to start. In the beginning, the most important thing is to get the framework onto paper. Rid yourself of the notion that your essay can be perfect on the first try. Perfection will require multiple drafts. Do not agonize over a particular word choice or fret over the phrasing of an idea. Simply get the ideas out of your mind and onto paper or a computer screen.

Creating an Outline

The easiest way to sabotage all the work you have done so far is to skip this step. Writing is as much a discipline as it is an art. To ensure that your essays flow well and make sense, you need to construct solid outlines before you write. Unless you conscientiously impose structure around your ideas, your essays will likely be rambling and ineffective.

Based on the information you have developed throughout the last chapters, choose one essay, and construct an outline that contains the central idea as well as its supporting points. At its most basic, an outline will be as simple as this:

Introduction (which contains the central idea)

Paragraph #1
    Topic sentence that ties into the central idea
    Supporting point #1

Paragraph #2
    Topic sentence that links the above paragraph to the next
    Supporting point #2

Paragraph #3
    Topic sentence that links the above paragraph to the next
    Supporting point #3

Conclusion (which reiterates the central idea and takes it one step further)

An outline should make sense on its own. The ideas should read logically in the order that you list them. Adding content around these main points should support and reinforce the logic of the outline. Finally, the outline should conclude with an insightful thought or image. Make sure that the rest of your outline reinforces this conclusion. The transition into the final paragraph is critical. If the committee members do not clearly see how you arrived at this final idea, you have either shoehorned a conclusion into the outline or your outline lacks focus.

You can take this simple outline structure and apply it to the material you have in many different ways. We hope your points and examples will fall into a natural and straightforward sequence on their own, without being forced. For ideas about how you might modify this general structure, read the examples of different essay categories below. See if your ideas fall naturally into one of the described structures.

Point for Point

This type of essay structures itself directly in response to the question asked. It is usually applied in response to questions that ask multiple things at once.

A good example of this type is the Why M.B.A.? question. You may be asked to describe in a single essay your past experience, short-term goals, long-term goals, reasons for wanting an M.B.A., and reasons for attending that particular school. When you are saddled with so many tasks at once, an easy way to organize your answer is to let the question itself become your outline. Answer each part of the question in the order it is asked, dedicating one paragraph for each response. Look, for example, at Essay 2. The writer's use of this structure can be easily spotted by looking at the first line of every paragraph:

Question: Specifically address your post-M.B.A. short- and long-term professional goals. How will Darden assist you in attaining these goals?

Paragraph 1: (answers short-term goals) "My short-term post-M.B.A. goal is to continue developing my general management skills while working in an intellectually challenging environment."

Paragraph 2: (answers long-term goals) "My long-term goal is to be the C.E.O. of a corporation, possibly my own."

Paragraph 3: (supports and explains goals with further evidence) "My new job as quality manager has convinced me that I should pursue a career in general management."

Paragraph 4: (answers why M.B.A.) "I believe that the entire M.B.A. experience will be central to my future success and achievement for two reasons."

Paragraph 5: (answers why Darden) "Darden will assist me in attaining my goals in many ways, but three characteristics of the school stand out to me."

Closing Sentence: (sums up and emphasizes final point) "In sum, I am applying to Darden because of its integrated curriculum, its focus on ethics and honor, and its impressive community of students and faculty."

Structural Segmentation

Another way to apply a structure to your essay using the question itself as a guide is to segment your essay into titled sections according to the number of points you plan to make. This is most often done in response to a question that asks for a specific quantity of examples. Examples include, "Discuss two situations where you have taken an active leadership role," or "Describe your three most substantial accomplishments." Many applicants choose to use structural segmentation because it legitimately eliminates the need to write an introduction, conclusion, and transitions. It can also save you from having to start with the tired approach of repeating the question in the first sentence like, "The two situations that I believe demonstrate my leadership abilities are . . . ."

Essays 12, 13, and 14 all demonstrate traditional uses of structural segmentation. Essay 14, for example, is segmented into two sections, "Teaching as a Teach For America Corps Member" and "Raising Funds for Teach For America." Essay 15, on the other hand, is less traditional. This writer does not use sections to demonstrate isolated points or experiences. Instead, he uses them to build action and create momentum for his opening story by using titles like, "The Lead-In," "The Situation," and "The Test."

Example Essay

This is a very traditional and useful type of essay that presents a series of specific examples to define and support the idea being communicated. This approach is one of the most common and can be used in response to almost any kind of question. Many questions call for this type specifically when they ask you to list a number of examples demonstrating a skill, ability, or accomplishment. Take a look, for example, at the organization inherent in Essay 34, keeping in mind that she has provided a specific situation to demonstrate every point:

Question: If we had met you five years ago and then met you again today, how would we say that you have changed? Include specific examples that characterize your development.

Paragraph 1: (sets up the scene) "Five years ago I was twenty years old, just finishing up my first semester of my sophomore year in school."

Paragraph 2: (answers how she has changed) "Now I live in a rowdy, crazy, colorful, slightly shady neighborhood in Washington, D.C. . . ."

Paragraph 3: (deepens exploration of change) "But the biggest changes have been in how I relate to my work and the people around me."

Paragraph 4: (first example) "I learned how to learn."

Paragraph 5: (second example) "I've learned to enjoy the small moments of joy that every day contains."

Paragraph 6: (third example) "I've learned to forgive myself."

Paragraph 7: (fourth example) "I've learned to be a positive member of the team."

Paragraph 8: (conclusion/summary) "In five years I've grown more confident, more secure, and more at ease. . . ."

Chronological

To facilitate smooth transitions, you might apply a chronological approach to your outline. The sequence of events will help reinforce flow from one stage of the essay to the next. One downfall of this approach is that you may create an essay that reads like a ship's log. Be sure that the element of time does not stifle the message you want to convey through the story. Do not feel obligated to tell more of the story than you need to convey your point adequately.

The chronological method does not have to span many years or even months. Essay 31 used it to describe a single event. The first lines of each paragraph show the chronology of the event:

Question: Describe an ethical dilemma you experienced firsthand. How did you manage and resolve the situation?

Paragraph 1: (sets up the situation in a general time scheme) "In late 1994 I worked on an equity offering for a Houston-based client with whom [investment bank] had built a very strong working relationship."

Paragraph 2: (begins the action at lunch) "This odd situation came to a head late in the deal during a lunch I attended in the executive dining room."

Paragraph 3: (moves to that evening) "I spent that evening in my hotel room wondering how I could, and if I should, continue working for clients with such prejudice. . . ."

Paragraph 4: (the next day) "The next day I discussed my concerns with the client manager, reminding him that [former chairman] had unequivocally stated the firm's motto as. . . ."

Paragraph 5: (jumps to the last weeks of the project) "True to my convictions, I did all of my work from New York during the last few weeks of this project. . . ."

Closing Sentence: (concludes with present day) "Appropriately enough, this client is currently under compliance review. . . ."

Narrative

This type of essay tells a story. A narrative essay can be structured in many ways. The chronological essay above, for example, is a kind of narrative. However, in its purest form, the narrative essay does nothing but tell the story. It begins and ends with the action. A more common use of the narrative approach occurs at the beginning of an essay as a means of drawing in the reader. Essay 15 does this by beginning with a hockey story. His first line takes us directly into the thick of the action: "I carried the puck up the left wing and couldn't find a teammate as I reached the offensive zone." He does not step out of the story until his last paragraph, which begins with the distancing and authoritative, "Leadership is not appointed, it is earned."

Descriptive

A descriptive essay is close to a narrative essay, but it appeals to the senses of the audience without necessarily drawing on the action of a story. This type of essay contains no inherent structure—it relies purely on vivid imagery and sensory detail. Take Essay 20, for example. It describes with a high level of acuity and detail the writer's personal experience of running: "My breath escapes my lungs in short gasps; I can feel my heart pounding in my chest to the rhythm of my shoes hitting the pavement; and although it's a brisk thirty-eight degrees outside, sweat races down my face." This essay is pure description from beginning to end. It is not a narrative essay because it does not tell a story or build to a climax. The power of this essay lies in its ability to leave the committee with a single, vivid image. Single images are easier to remember than a list of points, qualities, traits, or qualifications, no matter how impressive any one or all of them are.

Compare and Contrast

This essay usually depicts a before-and-after experience. Many questions specifically call for this approach. For example, the question in the previous example asks you to describe how you have changed during the last five years. The failure question, on the other hand, does not specifically ask for this structure. However, employing it can be a very good way to demonstrate how you have changed and learned from the experience. A well-executed example of this technique is Essay 28. The writer describes one experience that did not turn out well. She then pivots with the sentence, "After the disastrous turnout at Yale, I did the only thing I could do: make certain that the same thing didn't happen at Harvard." She then compares the first experience to a very similar one that ended in success.

This essay uses a block style. It thoroughly covers a point in the first half of the essay and then compares that point with another in the last half. You can also compare and contrast point by point, where specific situations are compared and contrasted one after the other. An example of this can be found in Essay 34:

Question: If we had met you five years ago and then met you again today, how would we say that you have changed? Include specific examples that characterize your development.

Paragraph 1: (introduces the subject) "In many respects, my life has changed dramatically in the past five years."

Paragraph 2: (compares/contrasts first point) "First, there is a marked contrast in my career focus between five years ago and today."

Paragraph 3: (compares/contrasts second point) "Another area of my professional life in which I have experienced tremendous growth is my ability to communicate and deal with many different types of people."

Paragraph 4: (compares/contrasts third point) "Finally, if you had met me five years ago, you would have found that my life goals were quite different from today."

Paragraph 5: (expands and expounds on last point) "My goals were to attain a comfortable life for myself, and to have time for my personal leisure. Since then, I have become a Christian. . . ."

Cause and Effect

Cause and effect is most often used in response to questions about influence and failure. It demonstrates that you know how to hold yourself accountable for your actions. In other words, "I caused this and know that I am responsible for the effect, which is. . . ." Additionally, cause and effect can show that you appreciate the effect other people and situations have on your growth, development, and maturity.

This structure can be used in many other instances as well. When used to respond to any question, cause and effect shows that you know how to take action and create change. Essayist 9, for example, tells how her father's sickness and subsequent death resulted in her passion for volunteering and philanthropy. Essayist 30 demonstrates the very similar effects of her reaction to the dilemma about the homeless situation. Both use the loose structure of *X* cause prompting them to take action to bring about *Y* effect.

Leading the Way

The emphasis on leading sentences in the previous essays should have demonstrated the importance of introducing the theme of each paragraph and reinforcing the structure of the essay. The most important leading sentence of all, of course, is the first sentence of your essay. The words and images you use must do more than simply announce the theme or topic of your essay—they must engage the reader. You do not want an admissions officer to start reading your essay and think, "Here we go again." If, after the first sentence, the admissions counselor does not like what she sees, she may not continue reading.

You do not have to begin by writing the lead. Often, you will spot the lead floating around in the middle of your first draft. You can use many different kinds of effective leads. You will find examples of some of them listed below. Remember, too, that if you have segmented your essay into distinct parts with different titles, you need to treat every segment as a separate essay and find an effective lead for each.

Standard Lead

Standard leads answer one or more of the six basic questions: who, what, when, where, why, and how. They should give the reader an idea of what to expect. A summary lead is a standard lead that answers most of these questions in one sentence. They often simply rephrase the question asked and are perhaps the most commonly used lead. Examples of three standard leads follow.

> *While I have had many opportunities to serve in the capacity of a leader in both my personal and professional lives, there are two occasions that I feel clearly demonstrate my managerial potential. (Essay 17)*

> *There are two individuals who have deeply shaped my professional thinking. (Essay 24)*

> *My most important cross-cultural experience is related to the fifteen months I spent in Thailand as a teacher of Economics and Business in a Cambodian refugee camp. (Essay 46)*

Surprise Lead

This type of lead attempts to shock or add interest. The following two extracts are examples of surprise leads.

During my senior year in college, my father was diagnosed with terminal skin cancer. (Essay 8)

Recently, I was trapped on a ledge more than 300 feet above the ground when an unexpected snow storm hit while rock climbing. (Essay 41)

Action Lead

This lead takes the reader into the middle of a piece of action. It is particularly useful in short essays, where space needs to be conserved, or in narrative/descriptive essays that begin with a story. An example of an action lead follows.

I carried the puck up the left wing and couldn't find a teammate as I reached the offensive zone. (Essay 15)

Commanding Lead

This lead presents a piece of impressive information about the writer in a commanding or authoritative tone. It conveys the image of a very confident, directed applicant. When employing a commanding lead, the rest of the essay needs to be made strong enough to back up the impression. The following extracts exemplify a commanding lead.

During the summer before my senior year, I founded and managed a company that employed five people and grossed twenty thousand dollars. (Essay 13, Segment 1)

In my senior year at Harvard, I led our ECAC champion hockey team in points, becoming the first player to ever begin his career on the J.V. team and finish as the varsity's leading scorer. (Essay 13, Segment 2)

I paid for the majority of my college education, while achieving Dean's List every semester, spent forty hours each week participating in a Division 1 athletic program, worked ten to fifteen hours each week to help defray tuition costs, and also maintained a balanced social life. (Essay 13, Segment 3)

Informative Lead

This lead gives the reader a fact or a statistic connected to the topic of your essay. It can also simply provide a piece of information about yourself or a situation. Examples of informative leads follow.

Technological innovation is occurring at an ever-increasing pace. (Essay 45)

Six months ago, my church implemented a new organizational structure in which all the various church functions were consolidated under the responsibility of one of ten different committees. (Essay 48)

Quotation Lead

This type of lead is most effective when the quote you choose is unusual, esoteric, funny or obscure, and not too long. Choose a quote with a meaning you plan to reveal to the reader as the essay progresses. Do not use a proverb or cliché, and do not attempt to interpret the quote in your essay. The admissions committee is more interested in how you respond to it and what that response says about you. The following exemplifies a quotation lead.

> *"It's in my blood, it's in my veins, I am the ghost who entertains."*
>
> —Peter Weiss, *Wie dem Herrn Mockinpott das Leiden ausgetrieben wird (Essay 22)*

Dialogue Lead

This lead brings the reader into a conversation. It can take the form of an actual dialogue between two people or can simply be a snippet of personal thought. The following are examples of dialogue leads.

> *Stop foolin' around, old boy. How would an M.B.A. help you? Better get on with your career. (Essay 1)*

> *First-rate skiing, the Winter Carnival, a bucolic setting, Ivy League football, and a great career at the end of it all? Who wouldn't want a Tuck M.B.A.? (Essay 3)*

Transitioning

The leads in subsequent paragraphs (those following your first) play the important role of transitioning. Writing smooth transitions between paragraphs is crucial to the flow of a good essay. Transitions provide an overall cohesiveness to your ideas. An essay without good transitions is like a series of isolated islands; the reader will struggle to get from one point to the next. Use transitions like bridges between your ideas.

As you move from one paragraph to the next, you should not have to explain your story in addition to telling it. If the transitions between paragraphs require explanation, your essay is either too large in scope or does not have a logical flow. A good transition statement will straddle the line between the two paragraphs, making your thoughts blend seamlessly like colors in a spectrum.

All of the examples used earlier in this chapter to demonstrate different essay types provide good examples of strong transitions. If the concepts in your outline follow and build on one another naturally, transitions will practically write themselves. If you are having trouble transitioning between paragraphs, you may have more of a structural problem, which you need to deal with in your outline, rather than simply a sentence structure problem.

Closing Your Case

The final sentence or two of your essay is critical. It must finish your thought or assertion. It helps create a positive and memorable image. Reading the ending is the last experience an admissions officer has with your essay. You need to make that moment count. A standard close merely summarizes the main points you have made. Do not feel obligated to tie everything up into a neat bow. The essay can conclude with some ambiguity, if appropriate, as long as it offers insights. If you have introduced a clever or unusual thought in the first paragraph, refer back to it in your conclusion. You want the admissions officer to leave your essay thinking, "That was a satisfying read," and "I wish the applicant had written more."

Essay 1, for example, closes with, "So I am not going to take my friends' advice. They have their dogs already, and the BMW is ordered. Sorry—I am not ready for that." This ending provides a strong, personal close. It reflects back on the writer's resistance to take advice and follow the usual path. The essayist opened with this theme in the first sentence when he wrote, "'Stop foolin' around, old boy. How would an M.B.A. help you? Better get on with your career.' That's what they say. Friends, colleagues, others. . . ." He reiterated the theme in the middle of the essay by writing, "Getting a dog at 35 and the BMW and house that go with it. No thanks. . . ." He could have easily ended with the previous paragraph. It sums up the points he made in his essay and is itself a good example of a standard close. However, by opting for a more lighthearted approach, he not only ties neatly back into his theme but also leaves the reader with a strong sense of his personality.

Essay 34 contains another example of an effective close. The last paragraph reads, "In five years I've grown more confident, more secure, and more at ease. I wouldn't say I'm a different person than I was at twenty, but I'm definitely an improved version. Plus—the biggest change of all—I'm a brunette now." The first sentence of this close provides the summary of the points previously made. The second reiterates back to the question asked. The third sentence is like icing on the cake. It not only ties back to an earlier allusion made in the first paragraph ("I had curly blond hair down to my waist. . . .") but also lets the reader finish with a smile.

Sentence Length and Structure

After you have written five or so solid paragraphs with attention-grabbing leads, good transitions, and strong conclusions, examine the pacing of your sentences. Are they all the same length? If so, vary their length and complexity. This is a good time to read your essays out loud. As you read, listen to the rhythm of the sentences. If each of your sentences twists and turns throughout an entire paragraph, try breaking them up for variety. Admissions officers do not enjoy reading essays that look like they were written with a thesaurus in hand. Forget the big words and dry, academic tone—remember that short sentences have great impact.

One way to determine whether you are using a variety of different sentence lengths is to write *S*, *M*, or *L* (for short, medium, and long) above each sentence in a paragraph. A dull paragraph can look something like this,

M M M L M S S S M L

On the other hand, an interesting paragraph may look more like this,

S L M M L S

Take a Break!

You have written a first draft and deserve a reward for the hard work—take a break! After you finish a draft, let it sit for a couple of days. You need to distance yourself from the piece so you can gain objectivity. Writing can be an emotional and exhausting process, particularly when you write about yourself and your experiences. After you finish writing your first draft, you may think a bit too highly of your efforts—or you may be too harsh. Both extremes are probably inaccurate. Once you have let your work sit for a while, you will be better able to take the next (and final!) step, which Chapter 5 presents, "Make It Perfect."

Make It Perfect

- The importance of revising your essay (again and again) cannot be stressed enough.
- Focus your first revision on substance alone.
- Assure that your essay is interesting, personal, and honest.
- Make sure that your essay is well structured and flows smoothly (use our structure test).
- Hunt for overuse of the passive voice and try to correct it wherever possible.
- Read your essay aloud to detect awkward language.
- Scour your essay for typos, grammatical and spelling errors, poor word choice, etc.
- Replace the school's name in all essays being sent to more than one school.
- Get Feedback!

Writing is not a one-time act. Writing is a process, and memorable writing comes more from rewriting than it does from the first draft. By rewriting, you will improve your essay—guaranteed. There is no perfect number of drafts that will ensure a great essay, but you will eventually reach a point when your confidence in the strength of your writing is reinforced by the feedback of others. If you skimp on the rewriting process, you significantly reduce the chances that your essay will be as good as it can be. Don't take that chance. The following steps show you how to take your essay from rough to remarkable.

Revise

Once you have taken a break away from your essay, come back and read it with a fresh perspective. Analyze it as objectively as possible based on the following three components: substance, structure, and interest. Do not worry yet about surface errors and spelling mistakes; focus instead on the larger issues. Be prepared to find some significant problems with your essays and be willing to address them even though it might mean significantly more work. Also, if you find yourself unable to iron out the bugs that turn up, you should be willing to consider starting one or two of your essays from scratch, potentially with a new topic.

Substance

Substance refers to the content of your essay and the message you are sending out. It can be very hard to gauge in your own writing. One good way to make sure that you have conveyed what you intended to convey is to write down, briefly and in your own words, the message you are trying to communicate. Then remove the introduction and conclusion from your essay and have an objective reader review what is left and do the same. Compare the two statements to see how similar they are. This can be especially helpful if you wrote a narrative, to make sure that your points are being communicated in the story.

Here are some more questions to ask regarding content:

- Have you answered the question that was asked?

- Is each point that you have made backed up by an example?

- Are your examples concrete and personal?

- Have you been specific? Go on a generalities hunt. Turn the generalities into specifics.

- Is the essay about you? (The answer should be "Yes!")

- What does it say about you? Try making a list of all the words you have used to describe yourself (directly or indirectly). Does the list accurately represent you?

- Does the writing sound like you? Is it personal and informal rather than uptight or stiff?

- Read your introduction. Is it personal and written in your own voice? If it is general or makes any broad claims, then have someone proofread your essay once without it. Did your proofreader notice that it was missing? If the essay can stand on its own without it, then consider removing it permanently.

Structure

To check the overall structure of your essay, do a first sentence check. Write down the first sentence of every paragraph in order. Read through them one after another, and ask yourself the following:

- Would someone who was reading only these sentences still understand exactly what you are trying to say?
- Are all of your main points expressed in the first sentences?
- Do the thoughts flow naturally, or do they seem to skip around or come out of left field?

Now go back to your essay as a whole and ask yourself these questions:

- Does each paragraph stick to the thought that was introduced in the first sentence?
- Is each point supported by a piece of evidence? How well does the evidence support the point?
- Is each paragraph of roughly the same length? When you step back and squint at your essay do they look balanced on the page? If one is significantly longer than the rest, you are probably trying to squeeze more than one thought into it.
- Does your conclusion draw naturally from the previous paragraphs?

Interest

Many people think only of mechanics when they revise and rewrite their compositions. But as we know, making your statement interesting is crucial in keeping the admissions officers reading and in making your essay memorable. Look at your essay with the interest equation in mind: personal + specific = interesting. Answer the following:

- Is the opening paragraph personal? Did you start with action or an image?
- At what point does your essay really begin? Try deleting all the sentences before that point.
- Does the essay "show" rather than "tell?" Use details whenever possible to create images.
- Did you use any words that you wouldn't use in a conversation? Did you take any words from a thesaurus? (If either answer is yes, get rid of them!)
- Have you used an active voice? (See more about this below.)
- Did you do the verb check. Are your verbs active and interesting?
- Have you overused adjectives and adverbs?
- Have you eliminated trite expressions and clichés?

- Does it sound interesting to you? If it bores you, it will bore others.
- Will the ending give the reader a sense of completeness? Does the last sentence sound like the last sentence?

The Hunt for Red Flags

How can you know if you are writing in a passive or active voice? Certain words and phrases are red flags for the passive voice, and relying on them too heavily will considerably weaken an otherwise good essay. To find out if your essay is suffering from passivity, go on a hunt for all of the following, highlighting each one as you find it:

"really"
"there is"
"it is essential that"
"nonetheless/nevertheless"
"in conclusion"
"yet"
"rather"
"it is important to note that"
"however"
"in addition"
"for instance"
"very"
"although"
"I feel"
"I hope"
"maybe"
"usually"
"have had"
"in fact"
"I believe"
"can be"
"perhaps"
"may/may not"
"somewhat"

When you are done, see how much of your essay is highlighted. You do not need to eliminate these phrases completely, but ask yourself if each one is necessary. Try replacing the phrase with a stronger one.

Proofread

When you are satisfied with the structure and content of your essay, it is time to check for grammar, spelling, typos, and the like. There will be obvious things you can fix right away: a misspelled or misused word, a seemingly endless sentence, or improper punctuation. Keep rewriting until your words say what you want them to say. Ask yourself these questions:

- Did I punctuate correctly?
- Did I eliminate exclamation points (except in dialogue)?
- Did I use capitalization clearly and consistently?
- Do the subjects agree in number with the verbs?
- Did I place the periods and commas inside the quotation marks?
- Did I keep contractions to a minimum? Are apostrophes in the right places?
- Did I replace the name of the proper school for each new application?

Read Out Loud

To help you polish the essay even further, read it out loud. You will be amazed at the faulty grammar and awkward language that your ears can detect. Reading out loud will also give you a good sense of the flow of the piece and will alert you to anything that sounds too abrupt or out of place. Good writing, like good music, has a certain rhythm. How does your essay sound? Interesting and varied, or drawn out and monotonous. This method also helps you to catch errors that your eyes might otherwise skim over while reading silently.

Get Feedback

We've mentioned this point many times throughout this text, but it can never be emphasized enough: *get feedback!* Not only will feedback help you see your essays objectively, as others will see them, but it is also a good way to get reinspired when you feel yourself burning out.

You should have already found someone to proof your essay for general style, structure, and content as was advised in Chapter 1. If you have to write multiple essays for one school, have someone evaluate the set as a whole. As a final step before submitting your application, find someone new to proof for the surface errors with fresh eyes.

As was said earlier, if you are having trouble finding someone willing (and able) to dedicate the time and thought that is needed to make this step effective, you may want to consider getting a professional evaluation. In addition to our own web site (*www.ivyessays.com*), a number of qualified services can be found on the Internet.

PART TWO

The Essays

A Guide to the Essays

The upcoming chapters contain over fifty business school application essays sorted by question type. We have included tips and advice at the beginning of each chapter to help you find the best approach to answer each question. The essays are not samples; they are real essays written by candidates accepted to the top schools. The name of the school that each candidate wrote the essay for (and was accepted to) is listed next to the essay number. You will also find some tags to help you quickly identify the essays that will be most relevant to you. Comments found after each essay can help you understand exactly why the essay worked by identifying the relative strengths and weaknesses of each.

This part preserves all of the mistakes, typos, grammar problems, and spelling errors found in the original essays. Despite these occasional surface errors, some of the most qualified applicants in the world wrote the essays. The quality of the essays, on the whole, is outstanding. Do not let this intimidate you. Use them as a learning tool and as a source of inspiration.

The following guide sorts the essays by some general category types. Use this guide as a fast way to target your search for the most applicable essays to your situation.

WORK EXPERIENCE

Consulting	1, 2, 17, 25, 28, 43
Entrepreneurialism	4, 13
Finance	3, 12, 31, 32
Management	2, 4, 25
Marketing	4
Military	10
Nonprofit	14, 30, 47
Politics/Government	24, 41
Publishing	5, 53
Teaching	14, 46
Technical/Engineering	1, 11, 16, 35, 45, 51

NONWORK ACTIVITIES

Athletes	9, 12, 13, 15, 20, 21, 29, 41
Entertainer	19
Humanists, volunteers, or philanthropists	8, 14, 18, 24, 33, 37, 40, 51, 55
Musician	55
Multiple activities	23, 36

MISCELLANEOUS

College (fraternity and sorority) life	9, 30, 55
Applicants with disabilities	41, 52
Family life/Influence	9, 38, 39, 40
Foreign applicants	1, 11, 12, 46
Gay applicant	54
International experience	1, 22, 46
Religious	35, 48

CHAPTER 6

Why an M.B.A.?

> - This question typically presents your first opportunity to make an impression.
> - Do not provide vague or general responses to this question.
> - Motivations should be clearly stated and evidenced by your experiences.
> - Your discussion of future career plans should convey focus and commitment.
> - Describing how a particular program fits into your plan will strengthen your position.

This is the most common type of essay question, asked on virtually every business school application. This question asks you to present, clearly and coherently, your all too familiar reasons for wanting an M.B.A. The questions usually consist of a few distinct parts. Most will ask about your past (How has your career progressed to date? What has motivated you thus far?), your future (How do you envision your career progressing? What are your goals for the future?), or both. All of them expect you to relate the information to your present desire to attain an M.B.A.

Since this is usually the first question asked, this essay will be the first one the officers see when they get your file. Let it create your first impression. It is similar to the moment in an interview when you shake the interviewer's hand and smile. Similarly, your first essay needs to be confident, direct, and to the point. The admissions committee uses this question to ascertain your motivation, maturity, and focus. While undergraduate application essays are understandably fuzzy about career choices and goals, graduate essays should, in contrast, be crystal clear. This does not mean that you must have every detail of your future mapped, but if you have vague reasons for pursuing an M.B.A., you need to reconsider your decision to apply. Giving a vague response to this question is akin to having a weak handshake and not looking the interviewer in the eye.

You must accomplish a lot in this essay, so pay special attention to structure. You can tackle the question by dividing your answer into three separate pieces. The first can be about your past professional experience. The second can discuss your future career goals. The third can be about the school's particular program. At each step, demonstrate why and how these experiences, goals, or attributes motivate you to get your M.B.A.

Limiting yourself to one career goal is best, if it is general. If you have a couple of different jobs in mind, that is all right too. However, your reasons for them should be easily inferred or specifically stated. If you are truly unsure of what your goals are (and we cannot talk you out of applying) always admit so honestly rather than fabricate. At the very least, though, give credible reasons for your indecision, and explain why you believe that this school's program will help you overcome your ambivalence.

Even if the question does not specifically ask for it, articulate why the particular program makes sense for you given your unique professional and personal goals. To do this well, you must spend the necessary time in introspection and also research the school. When you understand the school's program and positioning, use what you have uncovered only if you can apply it to yourself. Do not write what you think they want to hear. Admissions officers can spot this kind of insincerity. They also seek a heterogenous mix of backgrounds and experiences. Therefore, trying to fashion yourself after your conception of a typical applicant can hurt you even if you do it well. The truer you are to your real motivations and desires, the better your essay will be.

ESSAY 1: Wharton, high-tech consulting, physics background, European, experience in Asia

Discuss the factors that influenced your career decisions to date. Please describe your professional goals for the future. How will the M.B.A. experience influence your ability to achieve your goals?

"Stop foolin' around, old boy. How would an M.B.A. help you? Better get on with your career." That's what they say. Friends, colleagues, others.

I 've heard it all before. "If I were you, I would not do it. Don't waste your time, get ahead with your studies as quickly as possible", my professor for experimental physics told me. Of course he was not talking about my M.B.A., but about my intention to go to China: Take a special scholarship and go—for a year, to study Chinese, and physics, in China. Get in line, professor. He was just one of many who did not approve of my idea.

But for me, my plan clearly was: A chance, a challenge, and a choice. A chance to open my intellectual door to the world Europeans consider the (psychologically) most distant one from Western culture, and to broaden my view well beyond the usual. A challenge to learn a language Westerners see as one of the most difficult in a compressed timeframe and to adapt to a completely unfamiliar environment—while not letting this impact my overall physics studies timeline. A choice to diverge from the mainstream path to exclusive specialization in a single intellectual realm, not just on a spare time basis—but with serious commitment.

Looking back after seven years, I could not feel more assured that at that time, I made the right choice. My unusual combination of experiences sets me worlds apart from my physics-only ex-fellow students. Working for (Big Consulting Company), (so far) exclusively on international assignments in high tech industries, is the kind of job I had envisioned at that time. I could not have come here without that choice I made back then.

Now I am—on a higher playing field, though—back to square one: Once again, about to make an academic detour form the prescribed path. An unnecessary delay for my career progression.

But stop! Is that at all true? Getting an M.B.A. makes perfect sense for a consultant—after all, most consultants are M.B.A.s. Getting an M.B.A. makes even more sense in my particular case: it is the perfect academic supplement to my physics background—the one I need to become a leading edge high tech consultant. Detailed technology understanding plus profound business and group skills, that is a rare combination which really gets the career rocket roaring. This is certainly true for me, and I think that this is one of my most important and convincing reasons for an M.B.A.

Having spent considerable time and energy studying Chinese and travelling in Asia (and the rest of th world), an exclusively German career certainly is the opposite of what I am interested in. No cosy, warm place in an easy, totally predictable environment. Guaranteed career progression when the guy above me retires. Getting a dog at 35 and the BMW and house that go with it. No thanks.

So what is it I am interested in? I want to be where the guerilla wars of business are fought (the shoestring traveller resurfaces). Where global language and intercultural/personal skills make the difference. Where intelligence translates into quantum leaps (courtesy of the physicist). This is where I can make my best contribution. In short, I want to be where the action and the challenges are.

For the 21st century, this means, in terms of topic, clearly one industry: High Tech (just watch the stock market). I am well equipped for this with my physics background. In terms of region, it clearly means Asia. Through language study and travel exposure, I have come a long way in getting myself prepared. In terms of function, it clearly means strategy consulting. If there is any place better for this than (Big Consulting Company), please let me know.

Thus the reasons why I want to go back to university and do a dual degree in business and East Asian studies are: Get myself a thorough business background to put all the pieces of case experience I have accumulated during my (Big Consulting Company), life in their right places and understand their context. Do the same with all my pieces of Asian studies and travel experiences. Get ready for the real action I want to be a part and a driver of—and satisfy academic ambitions lurking beneath the surface of the "hands-on" consultant.

The knowledge I will gain should help facilitate a career change. After extensive work in European High Tech industry, I want to transfer to Asia. Completion of my desired academic program should give me perfect preparation, some initial contacts, and, through a summer internship in Asia, a clear idea of what to expect from working there (in contrast to studying and travelling).

Of at least equal importance, the Lauder/Wharton dual degree program will also give me a clear view on all the options that I have with my very special combination of skills. While I currently cannot imagine going anywhere else but to one of the Asian offices of (Big Consulting Company), after my graduation, I am also realistic enough to understand that there certainly is a number of other opportunities out there which I would be attracted to, but just know nothing about at this time. I am a firm believer in having many options and in exploring quite a few in detail—whatever position you're in, there may always be one which is an even better fit with your ambitions and capabilities.

I think it is obvious why I apply to the Wharton School. Among all the leading business schools, Lauder/Wharton is one of the very few offering a serious joint-degree program that makes sense. With its strong international orientation, Lauder/Wharton offers the type of courses I am looking for. With my diverse set of unusual ideas, experiences and capabilities, I would make a most valuable and colourful addition to the student body of Wharton.

So what are my concrete plans for the time after my graduation? Where in Asia can I be a driver the way described above? One extremely attractive option for me would be helping to set up the (Big Consulting Company), office in (Asian Capital). Or one in (Other Asian Capital). Or in Saigon (Cantonese and Vietnamese are no more different than Swedish and German). But frankly, these are just a few options I can pinpoint *now*—and I am sure that many more will become apparent during my Wharton experience.

After all, my desire to come to Wharton is just another manifestation of the characteristics that made me go to China a couple of years ago: Take the chance to widen your scope. Accept the challenge that goes with replacing narrow security by broad uncertainty. Make the choice to put all your effort into fully developing and playing out your talents.

So I am not going to take my friends' advice. They have their dogs already, and the BMW is ordered. Sorry—I am not ready for that.

Comments

The writer of this essay begins painting a picture of himself by discussing his trip to China. The fact that he took the trip instead of heeding all the advice others gave him shows determination, maturity, and character without him ever having to say the words. He clearly demonstrates why an M.B.A. makes sense for him generally (as a consultant) and specifically (to supplement his technical background). He pointedly bucks the usual stereotype of, "Getting a dog at 35 and the BMW and house that go with it." Instead, the essayist makes his reasons personal and unique by relating them directly to his professional goal of high-tech consulting in Asia. He then spends a paragraph specifically addressing the Wharton program. To demonstrate the sincerity and focused nature of his goals further, he lists a few very specific options that will be available to him once he graduates.

Certainly, his background and experience make him unusual. However, his style makes him stand out. The essayist consistently uses questions to transition to each new point without being distracting. He begins with a question. "Stop foolin' around, old boy. How would an M.B.A. help you?" Then he carries the theme throughout, "But stop! Is this all true?" and "So what is it I am interested in?" Finally, he writes, "So what are my concrete plans for the time after my graduation? Where in Asia can I be a driver the way described above?" To every question he asks he gives a succinct and pointed answer. He concludes by subtly reiterating his main points of chance, challenge, and choice. His last sentence adds the final stylistic touch by referring back to the question posed in the first sentence. In doing this, he effectively nails down the impression we have formed about his character without him ever having to espouse his own virtues directly.

The drawback of this essay is the grammar and mechanics. In parts, it was difficult to read due to punctuation errors and typos. The candidate had the right idea, but he would have benefited greatly from having a qualified individual iron out the kinks.

ESSAY 2: Darden, quality management, consulting

Specifically address your post-M.B.A. short- and long-term professional goals. How will Darden assist you in attaining these goals?

My short-term post-M.B.A. goal is to continue developing my general management skills while working in an intellectually challenging environment. Since graduating from college, I have always evaluated my work experiences by two criteria. First, I ask myself if I am learning, i.e. am I growing my knowledge base and am I becoming a brighter, more effective contributor to my business? Second, I ask myself if I am being challenged. Even if I am learning from my experience, if the pace is too slow, then I am unhappy. Obviously, no one wants to be overwhelmed and overcome by a surplus of unattainable objectives, but I am happiest when I am asked to stretch myself, to "take it to the next level." During my next few years in graduate school and in the workplace, I want to continue to push myself forward as I learn and grow as a student, as a business leader, and as a person.

My long-term goal is to be the C.E.O. of a corporation, possibly my own. My experiences in business have taught me two things which are driving me to attend graduate school in order to have the opportunity to achieve this goal. First, I believe that I will gain the most fulfillment and achieve the most success in a general management role rather than a functionally specific one. Second, I feel that business school is critical to attaining the knowledge and skills necessary to achieve my general management aspirations.

My new job as quality manager has convinced me that I should pursue a career in general management. As I oversee business processes cutting across departmental lines, I see how myopic a pure marketing, or human resources, or customer service viewpoint can be. The interplay between all departments within an organization is the key to success. In the face of any opportunity or challenge, if one department develops or changes without sufficient communication and coordination with the others, then whatever growth is achieved is compromised. I find managing and leading these interdepartmental relationships extremely rewarding.

I believe that the entire M.B.A. experience will be central to my future success and achievement for two reasons. First, the M.B.A. will give me the opportunity to rapidly develop the skill set needed to achieve my career goals. While it might be feasible to compile this knowledge without business school, I do not want to delay this personal growth imperative. Second, an M.B.A. will allow me to learn and to test myself in a very diverse and exciting environment. Just as companies know to benchmark externally to truly understand their potential, I know I will grow immensely by working, playing, learning, and competing with classmates who share a commitment to growth and a desire for achievement.

Darden will assist me in attaining my goals in many ways, but three characteristics of the school stand out to me. First, I am applying to Darden because of the integrated curriculum. As I have tackled the challenge of coordinating my company's process reengineering efforts, the importance of interdepartmental coordination and cooperation has become very clear to me. It is folly, indeed, to believe that the company can succeed if its internal departments view their success in internal terms rather than in terms of the entire company. In a similar fashion, the integrated curriculum must surely become more than the sum of its parts by virtue of the year-long coordination of the material. I believe that the integrated curriculum will provide the greatest return on my investment in learning. Second, I am applying to Darden because of its emphasis on ethics and the honor code. Achievements gained at the expense of fair play or honesty are tarnished, so I have always done whatever it has taken to achieve both my personal and professional goals with integrity. I expect to work very hard at business school and I want to do so in an environment such as the one which pervades Darden. Part of growth and development is the assumption of responsibility for actions and ownership of decisions; I see Darden's honor system as an embodiment of this principle. Finally, I am applying to Darden in order to surround myself with both students and faculty of the highest caliber, for I can imagine few fates worse than living in an unchallenging environment. Regardless of whether challenges come on academic, professional, or personal fronts, I believe that their associated problems and opportunities are the key to my development as a leader. I am confident that Darden's atmosphere is one full of healthy challenges which can lead only to continuous personal growth. In sum, I am applying to Darden because of its integrated curriculum, it's focus on ethics and honor, and it's impressive community of students and faculty.

Comments

This was written by a fairly typical M.B.A. candidate with a background in general management. Its superior organization and structure makes this essay strong. The essayist states his short-term goal in the first sentence of the first paragraph. He states his long-term goals in the first sentence of the second paragraph. His third paragraph demonstrates how his experience relates to his goals. His fourth answers Why an M.B.A.?, and his fifth and final paragraph answers Why us? Although his career goals and his reasons for getting an M.B.A. are both fairly typical, his treatment of Why Darden? stands out. The essayist shows that he has done his research by giving distinct reasons explaining why Darden suits him better than any other school. It offers an integrated curriculum and emphasizes ethics and integrity via an honor code. His final sentence summarizes and recounts these ideas, leaving the reader with the distinct impression of a logical, well-reasoned, goal-oriented individual.

ESSAY 3: Tuck, investment banking

Discuss your career progression to date. Why do you want an M.B.A.? How do you envision your career progressing after receiving the M.B.A.?

First-rate skiing, the Winter Carnival, a bucolic setting, Ivy League football, and a great career at the end of it all? Who wouldn't want a Tuck M.B.A.?

More seriously, I have given considerable thought to the qualities I seek in a graduate business program, and am convinced that Tuck is the very embodiment of the world-class business school. However, before I answer the question of why Dartmouth is my school of choice, I must first introduce you to my professional background and answer the question "Why do you want an M.B.A.?"

I chose a slightly different route from most accounting majors at Wharton. Instead of joining one of the Big Six accounting firms after graduation, I chose an investment bank. I did this because of an interest in financial services that arose from discussions with men and women in various industries, independent reading, and sheer fascination with the global banking network. In choosing a particular organization after college, I sought a firm with a reputation for excellence and rigor. First Bank had both these qualities in abundance.

I have been extremely pleased with my decision to come to First Bank. The training program to which I belonged encompassed a broad array of relevant topics, from foreign exchange trading and swaps accounting to managing diversity and business ethics. I have also been impressed with the assignments I have received and the steady increase in my level of responsibility. The specific project of which I am most proud involved the reengineering of the monthly Black Line Report (known as "the Line"), a lengthy report providing the confidential results of the Bank to senior management. When I first joined my current group, I thought the process we used to produce the Line was inefficient and the relevance of the information we were providing was questionable. I lobbied for the opportunity to investigate potential improvements. I was granted a small team of part-time and para-professional staff to help me improve the technical process. I conducted interviews with vice presidents and managing directors throughout the Bank to solicit their opinions and suggestions on the direction of the Line. I presented my ideas to senior management. My proposals for revisions to the Line with respect to both production and accounting policies were implemented almost in their entirety.

Through my training and work experiences I have developed important technical and management skills. I have created an extensive Bank-wide network and have received outstanding evaluations. Why, then, do I now wish to leave First Bank to pursue an M.B.A.? Because although I have an undergraduate business background and have graduated from a top-notch management training program, I recognize that my academic and professional education is not complete. My experiences at First Bank have been precious, but they have left me with one humbling self-assessment: I do not yet possess the tools that will be necessary to achieve my personal and professional goals.

When I observe senior managers throughout my firm, I marvel at their exceptional ability to lead their people and manage their businesses. I believe that inspired dedication and professional experience have contributed much on their road to success, but it is their superior technical skills and uncanny ability to lead that have been instrumental in their professional advancement. These two critical success factors of senior managers, technical knowledge and leadership abilities, have, for the most part, been acquired through higher education. I know I have the similar will to succeed and the maturity to learn from my experiences, but I still require the "M.B.A. Experience" to help complete the personal package that will ultimately lead to the attainment of my professional goals.

I have heard that the role of high caliber M.B.A. programs is to take people of varying backgrounds and interests and turn them all into investment bankers. Although I suspect the statement is hyperbole, I have in fact enjoyed a superb experience at an investment bank and will certainly consider banking as a career option. Still, given the exposure I would have at Dartmouth to a variety of career opportunities, I would not wish to limit myself to banking before exploring other industries. I do know that any position I accept will meet several specific criteria: the position will require the ability to readily adapt to changing conditions in the marketplace; I will be directly responsible for both the work and professional well-being of my subordinates; I will enjoy the freedom to implement reasonable changes that I determine to be in the best interests of the organization, its clients, or its shareholders; above all, I will thoroughly enjoy my job and the stream of new challenges it offers.

This leads me to the comparatively easier question, "Why Tuck?" Simply put, Tuck is the best match for my goals and interests. With an academic background in business and a C.P.A. certificate, I do not wish to further specialize in one area; rather I seek to hone my skills in a multiple of academic subjects and business disciplines. The Tuck curriculum caters to this desire. I am also convinced that Tuck can provide that critical bridge linking the theoretical and the practical in a manner that no other institution is able. What particularly excites me about Tuck is the profound sense of purpose and community. The small class-size, dormitory-style living, and rural setting all help to heighten the sense of team-spirit and collective achievement. Dartmouth's ties to the corporate community are also strong and venerable. The unparalleled devotion of Tuck alumni to their alma mater and their willingness to assist and counsel current students are strong indications that Tuck is indeed a very special place.

My Tuck education will act as much more than a mere tool for advancement. At Tuck I will learn from the finest students and faculty how to live and work in an environment that requires managers to balance successfully and delicately corporate needs with the needs of a diverse consumer population and labor force. I intend to be a manager respected for his ability to make quick and thorough decisions sensitive to the needs of various constituents, and I expect to attain such acumen in Hanover. Although not all of my post-M.B.A. career plans are definite, I know that the Dartmouth College Amos Tuck School of Business will invariably play a definable and pivotal role in the rest of my life.

Comments

This essay begins with a semi-risky approach. "First-rate skiing, the Winter Carnival, a bucolic setting, Ivy League football, and a great career at the end of it all? Who wouldn't want a Tuck M.B.A.?" If the essayist had not backed up this statement with a follow-through about the personal approach and seriously demonstrated his real motivations and qualifications, the opening would have seemed trite and posed.

His background in finance seems typical. However, he leverages his differences by pointing out that he is unique among his peers in combining an accounting education with experience in investment banking. He uses this as a springboard to discuss his success at First Bank, his leadership skills, and his initiative.

He answers Why an M.B.A.? with the following, common assertion, "I do not yet possess the tools that will be necessary to achieve my personal and professional goals." While he does point out a few general goals that he hopes to gain from an M.B.A., his specific goals are nebulous. Like the last writer, he does do a good job of specifying Why us? This essayist mentions several specifics, "Small class-size, dormitory-style living, rural setting . . . team-spirit and collective achievement . . . ties to the corporate community . . . unparalleled devotion of Tuck alumni . . . ." He is also frank about having indefinite post-M.B.A. career plans. This sincerity, combined with a simple, straightforward writing style and a personal touch, all combine to make this essay work.

ESSAY 4: Kellogg, marketing, management
Briefly assess your career progress to date. Elaborate on your future career plans and your motivation for pursuing a graduate degree at Kellogg.

I began my illustrious career at a bank more than three years ago. At that time, I had just graduated from the undergraduate program at the

Wharton School of Business; like most Whartonites, I thought I knew it all. If you had asked me then if I had any intention of returning to business school, I would have said that it was completely unnecessary for a person with such an incredibly keen grasp of the business world, as myself.

As it turns out, I was wrong. I've learned a lot since then. My first lesson was that no matter how hard I tried, I could never be happy as a banker. So two years ago, I decided to leave behind the world of banking in favor of something that I enjoy much more: the field of marketing.

I now market music, a product that engages people on so many different levels, both intellectual and emotional. I work for BMG, one of the largest direct mail companies in the country, and the decisions I make determine which C.D.s are mailed to our more than ten million members. The mathematical models I've designed have helped the segmentation department double its revenues to more than fifty million dollars.

In the last few years I've learned a great deal about the mail order business, statistical modeling, financial analysis and targeted marketing. But the most important thing I've learned—which I am still learning—is how to be an outstanding manager. Since being promoted from senior analyst to project manager, my responsibilities have grown tremendously. Before, I was solely responsible for the quality of my own work. Now, I must also manage and guide the work of others, certainly the most challenging and rewarding aspect of my new position.

I now directly supervise one junior analyst and coordinate the activities of a senior analyst in my department. I have learned to be a better teacher, motivator and leader. I know that these are the qualities which will determine my future success in business, and that I must pursue them in the most rigorous manner possible. This is why I have decided to return to school, and why I have chosen to apply to Kellogg.

The fact that Kellogg offers a Master of Management degree instead of the typical M.B.A. says it all. From the books I have read, the alumni I have spoken to, and the students I have met, one theme is reiterated: Kellogg is about people. Kellogg teaches you how to improve your leadership skills and work effectively as a team player, because that's what the real world is all about.

This teamwork approach combined with the school's first-class marketing department is reason enough for me to desire a Kellogg degree. Additionally, Evanston seems like an exciting place to spend a couple of years, with more than a score of clubs to join, from Business with a Heart to the Hash House Harriers. Finally, through programs like E-lab, Kellogg demonstrates its commitment to entrepreneurship. It is crucial that I master this discipline, since it plays an integral role in my future plans.

Following graduation, I hope to get a job in the strategic marketing department of an independent record label. In the course of a few years,

I hope to accumulate enough experience (and capital) to found a record label of my own, a label dedicated to artists with true talent, not merely commercial appeal. I know that I will need all of the leadership skills, technical expertise and friendships that I develop at Kellogg to help turn my dreams into realities.

These are the reasons why the J. L. Kellogg Graduate School of Management is my first choice.

Comments

In contrast with the last two essayists who have typical financial backgrounds, this writer boldly asserts, "No matter how hard I tried, I could never be happy as a banker." He begins with an eye-catching, not-so-positive portrait of himself as he was three years ago. The writer then describes how he has grown and changed since that time. The transformation from a stuck-up, over-confident banker to an informal, independent music lover sets him apart. The fact that he is in the business of marketing music helps his approach somewhat. This causes the committee members to expect someone who (pardon the cliché) walks to the beat of a different drummer. He builds on this by using an informal voice. ("Evanston seems like an exciting place to spend a couple of years, with more than a score of clubs to join . . . .") The writer combines this with serious business experience. ("The mathematical models I've designed have helped the segmentation department double its revenues to more than fifty million dollars.") He probably could have left off the last sentence, but the essay as a whole is strong enough to overcome this stylistic complaint.

ESSAY 5: Harvard, publishing
What are your post-M.B.A. career plans?

My experience working at Putnam Berkley has taught me a tremendous amount about the publishing industry and where I fit in.
I have discovered that I love publishing as much as I hoped I would. When I go into a bookstore and see our books on the shelves and understand the process that got them there, I am even more interested in them than before. I now eagerly check the spines to see which company published which book, evaluate the covers with a critical eye, and notice the book's placement in the store. Reading a "hot" new manuscript that has just come in from an agent isn't work; it's fun.

However, while I enjoy the challenge of editing, I prefer the other aspects of the business: seeing how to get books on the New York Times Bestseller list, learning about the complicated arrangements of advances paid to different authors, and understanding how the company makes money. And I now know that everyone in the industry has a say in which books get published, not just the editors.

I have decided that I want to get a more business-oriented job in publishing after graduation. Publishing is an old-fashioned industry, and most people have worked in it for their entire careers. People tend to do things the way they have always been done and are often unaware of alternatives. In a few short years, however, the industry is going to have to deal with a number of changes for which it is currently ill-equipped. The business is becoming increasingly complex as new channels of distribution (the superstores) are taking over from the independents, and electronic distribution and on-line services are becoming available and increasingly important. Even the very notion of what a publisher does will be challenged in the next few years. With electronic distribution of printed material possible, does the publishing company have a valid role? If so, what will it be? I want to be one of the people who helps answer these questions for the publishing industry.

Comments

This essay contrasts well with the other four in this group, because both the candidate and the question are atypical. The candidate has a background in the publishing field, an atypical background for business students. The question is atypical because it does not ask Why us? or even Why you? Rather it simply asks, What are your goals? This is one of Harvard's equivalents of the Why M.B.A.? question, and the university imposes a strict word limit on the answer. The writer has the right idea in presenting her goals and her reasons for these goals as concisely and pointedly as possible. This essay is refreshing. It discusses a field about which admissions committees do not usually hear. The essayist presents the changing field of publishing accurately. Her vision of her role in it (and her subsequent need for an M.B.A.) is credible.

ESSAY 6: Stanford

Why do you wish to earn an M.B.A. degree, particularly at the Stanford Graduate School of Business? How will the type of academic experience offered at the Stanford G.S.B. help you achieve your short-term and long-term goals?

I love success stories, particularly in business and sports. Much of my life centers around setting goals, pursuing interests, and achieving. As my career progresses, I will aggressively pursue upper management positions, particularly the role of CEO within a financial services firm, potentially my own. However, I recognize the value and significance of advanced preparation. The Stanford Graduate School of Business is an excellent arena from which to further develop my skills, allow exploration of our mutual interests, and pursue my career aspirations.

During my undergraduate education, proficiency in math and science led me initially into the engineering curriculum. However, business quickly won my heart. Living among dozens of business majors in my fraternity exposed me to economics, capitalism, and the financial markets. I quickly realized that creating wealth seemed much more appealing than creating electric circuits, for example.

After graduating from college, my work assignments began to build career experience. Fortunately, I found an opportunity to travel the country working for many different clients in a cash management consulting role for Ernst & Young. The position allowed me to use my analytical and interpersonal skills to identify technical opportunities for financial organizations to reduce costs or increase interest income. My work was rewarding—especially while uncovering million-dollar opportunities. However, my skill set became very specialized. Therefore, I pursued additional opportunities to work with multiple companies, but on a macro level.

Through personal and professional contacts I identified a career change to equity research, and earned a position with Morgan Stanley in New York City. The new role better fit my interests because of the broad exposure to many organizations and the financial markets. In research, I analyze publicly traded companies and make careful investment recommendations about their stocks. I relish the opportunity to evaluate firms on a high level, including calling upper management to discuss their strategic objectives and outlook. I take great pride in earning that job, which is often filled by M.B.A. graduates.

While gaining experience at Morgan Stanley, the long-term value of an M.B.A. degree became more apparent. In fact, when I joined the firm, I first noticed that the common educational background among upper management is an M.B.A. education. Specifically, the Associate Director of Research, whom I admire for his poise, strong leadership and intelligence, is an M.B.A. graduate. We visited about the virtues of an M.B.A. on several occasions and his perspectives and insight sealed my decision to earn a graduate business degree. He detailed both the tangible and intangible benefits that come with a general management degree from the Stanford G.S.B.: challenging academic work, strong professional relationships, and high impact managerial training.

My choice to no longer pursue a sell-side career fits perfectly with my future objectives. I have reached a natural decision point in my career. Given my experience and very successful pursuit of a C.F.A. designation (highest percentile of every category on Level I exam), a promotion to analyst as soon as next year is achievable. However, judging by precedent, further career advancement would likely be limited without a graduate degree. I will not allow a lack of higher education to limit my career progression, and fortunately, I enjoy academia. Thus, I am thrilled with the prospect of joining the Stanford community, developing my skill sets and unlocking new opportunities. At the same time, my experience gained advising and analyzing dozens of small and multinational companies will allow me to provide meaningful contributions to the classroom and community. The time for a Stanford M.B.A. is now.

Looking forward and building on the experiences gained from past job experiences, my short-term post-M.B.A. goal is to transition from the financial sell-side to the buy-side or private equity. This would allow me to continue to work in securities analysis in the medium-term, but at a multitude of firms outside of the New York area. These roles would satisfy my passion for work in the financial services arena, and enhance the pursuit of my ultimate career objective: to earn a leadership role in a financial services firm. However, I emphasize that an M.B.A. education is not necessary for my immediate advancement, but rather, the enhanced education is paramount to the skill set needed to achieve my long-term career aspirations.

This leads to perhaps the easier question: Why Stanford? As evident in my application, I am quantitative by nature. Consequently, I am seeking an education extending beyond self-taught financial formulas. I wish to supplement my financial expertise with strategic and managerial studies. Given the state of the world today, it is more apparent that we will demand strong, educated, and moral leadership to facilitate our country's growth. This is the training I seek. Fortunately, I believe the Stanford G.S.B. provides the learning environment ideally suited to address my personal, educational, and professional priorities.

Personally, the community environment created by the small class size is incredibly appealing. Coming from a small-town background, I appreciate the comfort level created by having personal relationships with each of your peers. In addition, Stanford's diverse student body provides a society of the most driven, successful, worldly individuals of my generation. Exposure to these future leaders provides a forum to broaden my horizon, develop the manner in which I relate to people, and enhance my ability to function within an environment of diverse influences. I believe the skills necessary to effectively integrate with co-workers and clients of various backgrounds are fundamental to being a successful businessperson.

Academically, the flexibility of Stanford's curriculum including the use of both lecture and case-study methodology, the ability to test out of courses, and the opportunity to pursue a concentration in finance while still reaping the benefits of a general management degree is very attractive. Though my career plans are focused on the financial world, I appreciate the opportunity to pursue classes on a variety of topics. For instance, I have demonstrated an entrepreneurial drive by previously starting two small businesses, and I would like to pursue this instinct further. So, especially intriguing to me is the entrepreneurship curriculum directed by Professor Irving Grousbeck. Former students rave about his courses.

Professionally, I relish the school's loyal alumni base with roots stretching deep into corporate America, particularly in private equity. As noted earlier, I am not necessarily pursuing an M.B.A. to reach my next position. More importantly, I hope to develop a skill set to earn significant future opportunities in which I can make great contributions. At that point, relationships with Stanford leaders across a wide range of institutions would prove highly beneficial.

The match between my aspirations and Stanford's multiple strengths provides an ideal fit and will help build my personal success story. Reciprocally, I intend to contribute fully to the academic community of Stanford University.

Comments

The applicant demonstrates his strong communication and writing skills in this essay. It clearly answers both questions posed, first Why an MBA, then Why Stanford. The candidate begins with information about his career experiences thus far, which leads into how an MBA will help him achieve his long-term career goals. After addressing this part of the question, he delves into why Stanford is the perfect fit. He has obviously done his research on the school, as he notes specific reasons for pursuing attendance.

Although the essay in general is strong, the last paragraph was unnecessary as it reads more like a forced summarization than a natural conclusion. The last sentence in particular is a dangler, offering no support to the claim.

ESSAY 7: Wharton WEMBA

What are your ultimate career objectives? How will the WEMBA program contribute to your attainment of these objectives? Why is this the right time for you to undertake this program?

Imagine you're 6 years old. Did you know what you wanted to be when you grew up: a fireman, astronaut, policeman, the President of the United States? I did, I knew exactly what I wanted to be. I wanted to be a doctor.

I was 6 years old when my dad first asked me, "What do you want to be when you grow up?" Since my first answer was Spiderman my dad was a little more persuasive and asked, "Don't you want to be a doctor and help people?" I took a moment to think and then said, "OK, I'll be a doctor." From that point on, I was going to be a doctor. Eleven years later, I stood at the doorstep to college ready to go into medicine. I didn't know anything about becoming a doctor, other than what I had heard—it was academically demanding, competitive and required an intense desire to succeed. So I focused on medicine and enrolled in UCLA's Biochemistry program.

During the next two years I became an avid student, not of medicine but of computers. I taught myself computer programming and worked my way through school. My professor put my initiative to work and we had a great symbiotic relationship. I learned technology and the Psychology department got their computer programs. After two years, it was apparent that I had fallen out of love with medicine. I decided that getting a degree in Biochemistry didn't make sense for me. Making the decision to leave UCLA was one of the most frightening but important things I ever did.

After leaving UCLA I spent the next five years searching for my true calling. I found that my love for computers made a decent living but didn't fulfill my creative desires, so I looked into other careers. My parents had been in entertainment, so I tried breaking into show business. I went to jazz school, took Shakespearean acting and learned screenwriting. But nothing seemed right—not entertainment, not computers, not medicine. Then I found Technical Resource Solutions (TRS).

TRS was a small technology consulting firm with an entrepreneurial spirit. I became great friends with the founders and soon the company was growing and so was my career. It was a great learning experience. I was on the front lines of business, working with a team who was determined to create something unique. Since TRS was so small, the culture was decidedly meritocratic. If you could do it well, you were assigned to the task. I worked across almost every area of the company spanning from technology to strategy to sales to marketing. I had finally found my niche: a place where I could use my drive and creativity to make a difference, while learning all along. Our small team became a determined family—going on sales calls, beating the big boys (we won contracts away from EDS and IBM), and doing a great job servicing our clients. I fell in love with the challenge of creating a company and building something from nothing. I had finally figured out what I wanted to do when I grew up: build a company. And just like medicine—it was demanding, competitive, required an intense desire to succeed and was creative and rewarding.

Then we hit a wall. Suddenly the company was just large enough to be doing well and we started losing focus. The executive team (myself included) became fragmented. We were on a plateau and couldn't figure out how to advance to the next stage. We wanted to go from being a good little company to being a great medium sized company but couldn't figure out how. The team was still able to battle with the big players but we weren't winning like before. Some of my best friends also worked for the company and they had become disenchanted and were leaving. It was a difficult time and we looked everywhere for answers. Was it the market? Was it the team? Was it our products? I had become a good manager and leader but I couldn't figure out how to move the company forward. Eventually we ended up merging with another company and stopped growing altogether. It was at that point that I took a good hard look at myself and although I was able to proudly say I was an excellent executive, there was something missing. In order to take the companies I worked for to the next level, I needed a solid foundation. That is when I decided to go to business school.

Just like thirteen years earlier, I didn't know anything about going to business school other than what I had heard—it was academically demanding, competitive and required an intense desire to succeed. But this time I focused and did my homework. I looked at my options and decided that in order to get the education, network, and skills I needed—I would need to go to an executive program from a school that would teach me not only the mechanics of business but would help me learn how to navigate the entrepreneurial rapids. A school that understood strategy, finance, entrepreneurship, leadership, and had the network to help me create a great company one day. It was a pretty tall order and I created a very short list: top twenty schools with executive programs well known for their all around capabilities. So I focused on business, went back and enrolled in UCLA's Economics program and found Wharton. The WEMBA program seemed tailor-made for my objectives. The M.B.A. would provide the academic foundation I needed across all business aspects and the Wharton reputation and network would provide me with the resources to build a truly great company and I could be part of a great alumni. It seemed a wonderful way to get into another business family, one that I could enhance with my determination and creativity.

It's now been twenty years since I started college. I have been involved in five different small companies and have proudly completed my economics degree. I once again have found myself on the doorstep to a new university. Except this time, I can finally answer "What do I want to be when I grow up?" And although Spiderman would still be a kid's dream, I want to be a builder—a really great company builder.

Comments

This is a refreshing essay. It breaks away from the norm in both style and structure. The author gets personal, allowing the admissions committee to get to know and like him. He opens with a story from his past—an introduction that is unique and interesting. He shares both academic and work experiences that allow the committee to see how he has evolved as a student and as a businessman. His future goals stem from a logical career progression, and he makes a strong case for why an MBA is the next reasonable step in his career path. He goes on to effectively convince the committee that Wharton WEMBA is the right program for him. The applicant showcased strong communication and writing skills while unveiling himself as a real person, not a statistic in a stack of applications.

CHAPTER 7

Contribution and Diversity

- This type of question demands a more personal response than many others.

- Consider using this opportunity to tell a story that reveals your personality.

- Topics may include talents, cultural diversity, or extraordinary personality traits (that can be supported by relevant experiences, of course).

- An effective response will explain how your distinctiveness will contribute to the school.

Every essay question on the admissions application is geared toward the same thing. Committee members want to find out who you are, what makes you different from everyone else, and how you will contribute to the school if accepted. This question asks these things outright. Because it asks so directly what the admissions committee wants to know, this is one of the most common questions you will find. The question has a structure similar to the Why M.B.A.? question. It asks both Why us? and Why you? However, the nature of this question lends itself to a more personal response. Whereas the Why M.B.A.? question asks what you have done, what you want to do, and how that relates to the school, this question asks about who you are and how it relates to the school. The Why M.B.A.? question asks about your experiences, and this question asks about your qualities.

Just as you brainstormed about your experiences, actions, and goals for the first question, brainstorm about your qualities and characteristics for this one. What sets you apart from everyone else? What words do friends and family use to describe you? For some people, the focus of this question will come easily.

A member of a minority can choose to focus on his or her racial or ethnic differences. A person with an unusual professional background may use this question to turn this potential weakness into a strength. Anyone with a particular talent or calling, such as an athlete or a musician, can use that as a topic. Less obvious characteristics can work just as well. Are you one of those people who are forever getting tagged with an identity? Do people say, "You know Chuck, the funny one," or "There's Jane, the history buff."

If you consider yourself to be a fairly typical candidate with a broad range of interests, you may feel nervous about not being able to identify yourself with any one particular activity or defining trait. You should not be worried. Describing the combination of qualities that make you unique is perfectly acceptable. None of your qualities has to be particularly unique by itself—whatever is real and true will work perfectly. What words do people use to describe you? Are you a risk taker? An academic? A leader? Unusually goal oriented? Dedicated? Ethical? A good team player?

The qualities you choose to describe are not nearly as important as how well you back them up. Because this answer tends to contain many adjectives, you absolutely must provide solid examples demonstrating each quality you have listed. You can take examples from either your work or your personal life. You can even be creative and take an example from your childhood, if you wish, as long as whatever you choose effectively proves that you are what you say you are.

Because this question asks "How will you contribute to our school?" it provides you with a perfect opportunity to prove that you have researched and targeted yourself to the particular school. Match your distinctiveness in whatever way is natural to the distinctiveness of the program. Show the admissions committee that you are not just perfect for business school in general, you are perfect for their business school.

ESSAY 8: Kellogg, hospital volunteer
Your background, experiences, and values will enhance the diversity of Kellogg's student body. How?

During my senior year in college, my father was diagnosed with terminal skin cancer. Like most cancer patients, he spent the majority of his time in the hospital; he often spoke of how nice the staff was, and how much his stay was enriched by the services offered by the volunteers. I felt a great debt to those people who helped my father and mother during that difficult time, and I wanted to do the same for other people in similar situations.

When I moved to New York after graduation, I decided to volunteer at the Sloan-Kettering Memorial Hospital until I found a job. Over the next few months, I worked thirty hours a week helping patients and their families. One of the most rewarding experiences at the hospital was organizing patient voting for the Presidential election. I was responsible for coordinating the procurement and distribution of absentee ballots with nurses, patients, hospital staff, and the various voting administrations within the five boroughs of New York City.

The response was overwhelming. The patients were overjoyed to be included in the voting process. I knew from my father that the most demoralizing circumstance of a prolonged hospital stay was the feeling that the world was passing you by. On that November day, however, I was able to help those patients feel like part of society again. I will always be grateful for that.

Once I found a job, I had to curtail my hours at the hospital, but I did not stop my volunteer work. And although my job prohibits me from volunteering as much as I'd like, I still try to find the time. My volunteer work has allowed me to help others cope with the terrible pain of illness, which I have experienced first-hand and through my family. The satisfaction that I gain when I help patients and their families is unlike any other feeling I have ever had in my life.

I've found that my work also helps me to deal with and accept the loss of my own father. If it were not for him, I never would have started volunteering. The good work I do is a constant tribute to his memory.

As an individual, I have learned the benefits of altruism, and I firmly believe that companies should also take an active role in philanthropy. I was pleased to see in the admissions brochure that other Kellogg students feel the same, as demonstrated by their Business with a Heart program. I know that my unique perspective and experiences would contribute to this group, and enable me to enrich the lives of the community as well as those of my fellow students.

Comments

This essayist is a good example of someone who chose to focus on one trait rather than several. By choosing only one quality, her essay is concise, to the point, and easy to read. She also leaves a strong impression by introducing only one theme. This essay is particularly strong because the writer does not simply label herself as a volunteer and leave it at that. She makes the topic personal. First, she walks us through her motivation, then through the experience itself, and finally through how it has affected her and made her different. She gives details to bring each of these steps alive but manages to do so in a very short amount of space. She even specifically details how this experience will help her contribute by listing the name of the program she has targeted.

ESSAY 9: Darden, triathlete, fraternity president, stepfather's influence

The Darden School seeks a diverse and unique entering class of future managers. How will your distinctiveness enrich our learning environment and enhance your prospects for success as a manager?

Different people, events, and situations in my life have shaped who I am today and the distinct blend of these influences has made me the individual I am. Three major influences, I believe, have contributed to my development and positioned me for success both as a student and as a manager. First, my experience in triathlon has taught me a great deal about who I am. While competing at the top level of the sport, I have learned much about my capabilities to remain focused over time such that I can compete and, win or lose, improve in order to be the best I can be. Second, my tenure as president of my college fraternity, Kappa Sigma, gave me my first opportunity to take a true leadership role, one where I was empowered by my peers to impact the lives of others and have a beneficial influence on my community. Finally, my step-father, Dean, has been for me a role model exemplifying all of the personal characteristics that I aspire to develop. Dean has been for me a shining example proving that excellence and achievement can and, in fact, must go hand-in-hand with ethical integrity. These three influences have, I believe, made me unique and predisposed to future success as a manager.

On October 15, 1994, I competed in the Ironman Triathlon World Championships, a triathlon consisting of a 2.4 mile swim, a 112 mile bike, and a 26.2 mile run, and set in a location, Kailua-Kona, Hawaii, noted always for its physical beauty and, one day each October, for its incredible demands on the human body. There are two distinct parts of competing at Ironman: First, you must get there. Second, you must race. Racing is the easy part. In 1994 I was one of approximately twenty American men aged 20–24 years who qualified to race in Hawaii.

Competing at triathlon's highest level has taught me focus, balance, and discovery. Focus because I could not achieve sufficient mental and physical strength without a complete and specific vision of the goal and the desire to achieve it. Triathlon has instilled in me a belief that there are no limits to what I can achieve if I am able to focus all of my energies on the ultimate objective. At any given time when you are pursuing an objective, distractions abound and present themselves as possible excuses for less than perfect performance. As I ran out of the bike-to-run transition area at Hawaii, I was beginning a marathon after six hours of racing. At that time, you can not help but question your ability to finish what you have begun. For me, this transition is always an important moment because it requires that I look beyond any pain I may be feeling and focus on my ultimate objective, the finish. I have found that continually pushing through this point in races has enabled me to push through difficult times in all aspects of my life. No matter what the barrier or obstacle, no matter how strong or plentiful my doubts may be, I know that I need only focus on the finish to succeed.

Balance because I must constantly measure the demands of my professional life against the demands of sport and because I must distribute my effort and time across the three disciplines of triathlon. Competing in Ironman distance triathlons requires a dedication which could easily detract from the other personal and professional aspects of my life, so I must be able to recognize when I am following one pursuit at the expense of others. I am, of course, constantly trying to find that twenty fifth hour in the day, but I am always forced to concede that I must instead make more out of the twenty four hours available. I have found that the key to balancing my different pursuits and achieving success therein is to see them not as competing objectives but rather as complementary ones. Just as running can develop aerobic fitness which can benefit cycling, triathlon can benefit me in ways which carry over to other aspects of my personal and business life and vice-versa.

Discovery because triathlon's demands have revealed my deepest strengths and weaknesses. In order to compete in races which can last ten hours and which sometimes contain just enough danger to make you worry, you have to be willing to face defeat. The key to continuing success, I believe, is the willingness to accept defeat as part of a larger process of growth. Whether your goal is to win the race, win your division, or set a personal best time, success is never guaranteed. Constant success would imply a lack of competition or insignificant goals. In either case, success would be empty and meaningless. I always expect to succeed, but when I don't I try to look within myself and identify where I fell short, what obstacles thwarted me, and where I did well but could have done better. Sometimes this process of introspection is painful, but it is the best way to bring meaning and purpose to defeat or failure.

During my junior year at Brown University, I led my fraternity, Kappa Sigma, through a period of great change which saw the house regain on-campus housing, increase membership, and renew its image. The prior year, Kappa Sigma had reached the nadir of its existence. Membership was down, the house was viewed as a negative influence at Brown, and the house had lost campus housing.

As the newly elected chapter president, I initiated a year-long program of broadened social activity, charity work, scholastic involvement, and membership growth which culminated in the complete resurrection of Kappa Sigma. The fraternity became positively active in the community, eventually winning an award for charitable fund raising. We actively promoted study groups and encouraged academic achievement within the membership. We drew an enormous, high quality pledge class by positioning Kappa Sigma as a unique opportunity to become involved in the birth of a fraternity which demonstrated the qualities desirable in campus leadership. It is always with a sense of great pride and accomplishment that I look back and realize that we were able to work together, refocus our goals, and become a positive leadership force on the Brown campus.

My experience as president of Kappa Sigma was significant to me because it marked the first time in my life when I was able to take a significant leadership role where I was able to impact the lives of others and benefit the community. When I was elected president of Kappa Sigma, the house had lost what made it so important and valuable to our members. Campus housing had been revoked, the public image was negative, and social opportunities were limited at best. What struck me most was the feeling that a very important aspect of life at Brown had been taken away from our membership and that I had the opportunity to help bring it back, to help restore Kappa Sigma to full strength.

My step-father is the single person who has had the greatest influence on my life. I first met Dean when I was fourteen years old and living with my mother, who had divorced when I was three. I had not been in contact with my father for two years, so Dean had the opportunity to fill a significant void in my life.

The single character trait of Dean's that I find most admirable is his ability to strive for and achieve excellence while never making any moral or ethical sacrifices. In Dean's case, this trait was evidenced at a very young age when he earned his Eagle Scout badge. Three decades later, when he was awarded an honorary doctoral degree, Dean still listed being an Eagle Scout as one of his life's major achievements. Today I see evidence of this trait in the manner in which his employees and friends treat him and refer to him. Whenever I have visited his office, I have always been impressed by the warmth and admiration expressed about Dean. As president of a major corporation, he is, after all, "the boss." It would be understandable if someone respected Dean, but did not like him. I have yet to meet that person and I don't think I ever will. In more personal settings, I have never met a friend of Dean's who did not respect and admire him. It seems that no one could resent him despite his numerous achievements, because he does not barter his morals or ethical principles for the sake of expediency.

I know that I share with Dean the desire for excellence along with the belief that anything achieved at the expense of fair play or honesty is a tainted achievement which holds no real value. In my personal and professional pursuits I have always been willing to do whatever it has taken to achieve my goals within that framework. Whether training for and racing in Hawaii, helping to lead my fraternity, or meeting my business objectives, I am never satisfied unless I put forth my best effort. It is not enough for me to simply meet a challenge; I feel the need to always strive to exceed any and all expectations in an effort to push myself as far as I can. I like to think that this trait is what has lead my peers to often elect me to lead team efforts I have been a part of. Did my fraternity brothers know that I would not stop short of fully restoring Kappa Sigma's status? Did my coworkers know when they chose me to lead my company's reengineering effort that I would be unwilling to let our effort fall anywhere short of success? I hope they did. It is certainly my aim to fulfill those expectations for they are my own. But as I have pursued these objectives, I have refused to take any shortcut which might compromise the integrity of those achievements.

Competing in triathlon, leading my fraternity, and knowing my step-father have all contributed strongly to my growth and development as a person. Triathlon has taught me a great deal about myself. I know what it takes to succeed and I know how to manage through any challenge as I focus on meeting my ultimate goals and objectives. Leading my fraternity gave me my first opportunity to lead a large group of people. I can never forget how much I grew and thrived in an environment which allowed me to positively influence the lives of others and give back to the community at large. I am proud to say that through it all I have followed the example given to me by step-father. I have led by example and I have done so with integrity. I have set only the highest expectations of myself and I have endeavored to meet them without ever sacrificing my principles for the sake of convenience. I am committed that as I go forward with my work, my schooling, and my life I will continue to be true to this ideal. With my background, my achievements, and my commitment to fair play and honesty, I have no doubt that I can contribute positively to Darden's environment and move forward into a successful managerial career.

Comments

The fact that this applicant is an Ironman triathlete gives him an automatic advantage in answering this question. That the writer does not rely on his physical achievement alone to set him apart makes this essay impressive. Instead, he clearly specifies what and how his experience has taught him. These qualities (focus, balance, and discovery) make the applicant different. However, he does not stop there either—he lists two more factors beyond his athleticism to demonstrate his potential as a contributor.

Despite the impressiveness of all that the essayist has done and the organized manner in which he has presented it, this essay is not perfect. He could have targeted the question better. Clearly, the writer used this essay to answer an influence question at another school and simply made the essay fit here. He could have easily changed the focus of the first paragraph from influence to distinctiveness, but he did not go the extra step. The fact that he did not says to the committee that this school was probably not his first choice.

ESSAY 10: Kellogg, Army officer

Your background, experiences, and values will enhance the diversity of Kellogg's student body. How?

As an officer in the U.S. Army, I have developed strong leadership skills and a deep commitment to public service. The Army places great emphasis on these characteristics, and after four years at West Point, and over four years as an officer, I have internalized both of these traits. If accepted to the J. L. Kellogg Graduate School of Management, these are the two most significant characteristics that I will bring to enhance the academic environment of my classmates.

Leadership in the Army is much more than the simple management of employees. An officer is responsible for not only the work performance of his soldiers, but also for their personal lives and general welfare. To lead soldiers is to be a father, priest, income-tax advisor, confessor, and judge to all of them at once. The trouble a young private can find fresh out of boot camp and away from home for the first time is a continuous source of amazement. Young families struggling on modest Army wages encounter all sorts of financial problems, and this is another area that demands significant attention. "Taking care of the troops" is almost a mantra in the Army, and you quickly learn that the duties of an officer go well beyond the job description. I enjoy helping soldiers and I have always found that the benefits to the unit are worth much more than the time invested. Employees who know that they have the support of management not only stay more focused, but they also develop a level of trust and loyalty that benefits the organization in many different ways. This is an essential aspect of good management, and I feel fortunate to have learned this early in my career.

Another aspect of the Army that makes good management skills essential is that an officer can not use direct compensation to reward and motivate subordinates. I often found it frustrating to be in charge of an organization and yet have no real control over either the salaries or the advancement of its members. With salaries determined by Congress, and promotions decided by a centralized committee, a commander in the Army must rely on the more subtle aspects of leadership to be effective. Good leadership is based on mutual respect, and I have found that it is much more effective to have the trust and confidence of your subordinates than to use direct compensation as the primarily tool of motivation. The ability to work with and motivate all different types of people is the greatest attribute I have gained through military service. The Army has exposed me to the fundamental and more human demands of effective leadership and this experience will be one of my contributions to the academic environment at Kellogg.

A strong commitment to public service will be another characteristic that I will bring to graduate school. West Point and the Army are marvelous institutions from which to learn the virtues of public service. Coming of age in an organization that holds duty and service to nation above all else has had a profound influence upon my life. The Army has educated me, solidified my moral character, and taught me how to lead. For this I am in debt to my country, and although I have ended my military service, I am committed to serving the common good throughout my business career and plan to someday return to direct public service.

As an officer in the Army, I have developed strong leadership skills and I have learned that to be most effective a manager must stay focused on the human aspects of leadership. I have also developed a strong commitment to public service, and I firmly believe that it is the duty of all professionals to ensure that their organizations function in support of society and not against it. I will be pleased if I can impart at least some measure of these convictions to my classmates at business school.

Comments

This is a good example of an applicant who chose to write about two commonplace characteristics (leadership and commitment to public service) but backed them up with real and unusual experience. In addition, this essay is very well structured, focused, and easy to follow.

Essay 11: Yale, Russian, hi-tech consulting

A person, who is beginning his management career, has no right for a mistake choosing a business school. I have chosen the Yale MPPM program as the most appropriate and promising bridge between my past and future, my experiences and my goals.

My professional goals are quite clear to me. I see my long-term professional goal in becoming an executive officer of a key hi-tech company. To reach it I have set my intermediate goals, which lead me to Strategic Alliances department of a major computer company. But I still lack some important management experiences and skills. So, to ensure success of my career I apply to the Yale SOM—a top quality business school able to provide me with opportunities to gain the knowledge I need for my future, ensure my perception of American values, and put me in contact with diverse student environment.

I am especially attracted by Yale student body, with its currently 38 nationalities. According to my experience, nothing contributes to the quality of education as much as diverse views and approaches of classmates. Yale MPPM curriculum ensures my progress in Finances and Accounting, Marketing, and Organization Behavior. It also promises such vital for my career courses as "Product Planning and Development", "Operations Management", "Competitive Strategies", and "Managerial Negotiations". The opportunity to benefit from the expertise of other departments of the University opens for me the path for becoming a manager of the most required type—open-minded, multi-disciplinary problem solver.

The "public-related" part of the program fixed my choice on Yale MPPM at once, as hi-tech industry is being more and more affected by political events and long-term consumer interests. In recent years this industry itself started affecting the society, determining advantages and disadvantages of social groups and whole nations, influencing the democratic processes. As a future decision-maker I should get ready for this responsibility too.

These are my expectations and study goals at Yale School of Management. However, I am coming to Yale not only to consume, but also to contribute. I shall bring to Yale SOM traditional Russian appreciation of teamwork—key quality for success in business and studies. I shall share with my classmates first-hand knowledge of many dozens of Russian businesses and my understanding of corporate business practices—a broad base for discussions and analysis. I shall also contribute my knowledge of computers and expertise in Management Information Systems of any scale (I seriously doubt that there is another applicant with comparable experience in this area). I foresee, that making my experiences available to others will also contribute to my growth, as I shall review them with people of many different backgrounds. As a result, my own perception of those experiences will become wider and deeper.

I have chosen Yale School of Management, because its features, unique even among top-rated M.B.A. programs, guarantee me an opportunity to reach my learning goals. I also chose it as a program, that incorporates high moral values as part of the curriculum, thus becoming a banner, which I shall carry with me throughout my career with honor. I believe, that years in Yale SOM will be a critical step in achieving my professional goals, a major step on my way into the future.

One's individual perceptions are the most untrustworthy indicators of his real contributions, especially when they cover such personally intangible qualities as sense of humor and intelligence. So I shall report in this essay those of my contributions, which are supported by clear evidence, and I shall just mention those which are not.

Up to now my influence on different organizations has been determined by my adventurous attitude to challenge. Life should be versatile to be interesting. So I do not avoid tougher assignments, and I look for new, unusual solutions where possible. In many cases it results in more efficient schemes of operations and new products. For instance, while working in [major computer corporation] I met a problem of insufficient technical service staff. Instead of encouraging the growth of service group, I managed to persuade remote customers to educate their own people. I took the trouble of developing and running personally (not being a professional instructor) a special technical service course. As a result of these actions customers' out-of-order periods decreased by two times, and [major computer corporation] avoided non-productive expenses.

Challenging spirit encourages me to work hard to reach professional excellence. I am always willing "to walk an extra mile" (even if it requires me to travel sitting on coffins in a cargo plane, as it happened once). This attitude normally results in higher quality of the projects, where I participate. For example, while creating software complex for the Aerodynamics Laboratory at Moscow Aviation Institute, I insisted on user-friendly interface. I am very proud that, due to my victory in that discussion, my system is still used without intervention of any support specialists.

My last employer [major computer corporation] East Europe/Asia benefited much from my ability to learn fast and progress simultaneously in several areas. Instead of keeping several underloaded specialists [major computer corporation] just provided me diverse education, so that very soon I was covering the most diverse product line in the whole service department: from office printers to [major computer corporation] supercomputers.

In the last five years I started paying more attention to self-management. It suddenly led to increase not only in my personal productivity, but also in efficiency of organizations, where I applied my skills. My achievements in establishing customer service procedures were valued by my [major computer corporation] managers and lead to my promotion to the position of Team Leader.

Another my valuable contribution is the traditional Russian team spirit. Many times in my career the investment of time and effort into support and growth of cooperation resulted in superb achievements. As a team leader in [major computer corporation] I initiated closer experience exchange in my group, and the united expertise gave us more than months of dedicated learning could do.

Challenging and creative state of mind, ability to learn fast, striving for professional excellence, team spirit and willingness to cooperate, strong self-management—these are my most contributing qualities. I also believe, that my friendly disposition to people, sense of responsibility, and my desire for improving this world, do add something valuable to the atmosphere around me. I rely on these sides of my character as a valuable support in my future career. I am taking them with me to Yale School of Management to add to its learning environment and creative spirit.

Comments

This candidate takes a different approach from the rest by spending the first half of the essay focusing on the school and the second half focusing on himself. The sometimes awkward phrasing is attributed to his status as a foreign applicant and is not prevalent enough to hurt him. Refreshingly, he did not rely on his foreign or technical background as the source of his distinctiveness. Instead, he chose some personal qualities such as his "Adventurous attitude to challenge," "Self management," and "Russian team spirit" and included his foreign and technical background to back up these qualities. His essay also has a refreshingly personal and informal tone that, according to the admissions officers we consulted, is rare to find in essays written by foreign applicants.

CHAPTER 8

Accomplishments

- Do not make a list of accomplishments to answer this question.
- Focus on an accomplishment that was truly meaningful to you.
- Use this opportunity to tell a story about yourself.
- If describing an accomplishment that is already listed on your application, make the discussion personal and interesting.

Your answer to this question will say a lot more about you than simply what you have accomplished. It will show the committee what you value, what makes you proud, and what you are capable of accomplishing. Applicants make a common mistake when answering this question—they repeat information found elsewhere in the application. A good student, for example, will be tempted to fall back on stressing his or her high G.P.A. or G.M.A.T. score. A person who has won a number of awards or acknowledgments will try to include all of them and end up turning the essay into little more than a prose list. Many of the questions specify that you choose one, two, or three specific accomplishments as a way of avoiding this kind of response.

If you do choose an accomplishment that the committee is already aware of— such as your induction into Phi Beta Kappa or a promotion that appears on your resume—then bring the experience alive. Demonstrate what it took to get there and how it affected you personally. Do not be afraid to show committee members that you are proud. This is not the place for modesty. However, do not fall to the other extreme either—you can toot your own horn, but do it without being didactic or preachy. You will not have to worry about either extreme if you keep your essay short and to the point. Spend the bulk of your essay simply telling the story.

If you are having trouble choosing something to focus on, then remember that the best essays are often about modest accomplishments. What you accomplished does not matter as long as you found it personally meaningful and can make it come alive. Unless specified, the accomplishment can be professional, personal, or academic. Did you get a compliment from a notoriously tight-lipped, hard-driving manager? Did you lose the race but beat your own best time? As an English major, did you work around the clock to bring a C in physics up to an A? Do not think about what they want to hear—think about what has really made you proud.

ESSAY 12: Columbia, European, banking, surfing

Describe the two accomplishments that occurred in the last five years of which you are most proud.

Strategic Advisory for American Savings Bank

In January of last year, my group was engaged by Robert Bass' Keystone Partners to evaluate their investment in California company, the culminating point of a five-year banking relationship. Keystone Partner however, engaged Goldman Sachs as co-advisor, thereby infuriating the Lehman team. We swore to keep control of the valuation process by solely handling the modeling work including complex simulations and projections, which I was solely responsible for. I quickly drafted a couple of pages that I distributed to both teams. Overnight, the Goldman team reproduced them line by line and sent them directly to the client as their work. It was a great strike against our team. I decided to design a completely different model, and to draw upon the information that I could gather from a long and fruitful client relationship with Lehman Brothers. I convinced the senior vice president, vice president and associate who had covered the company for years to pass on their knowledge, persuaded them to be available for 36 hours straight to answer all my questions, and for four more hours to be trained by me on the model. I designed a 23 page model, stuffed with information, that we presented to the 42 person working team, gathered at our request. The presentation, led by myself for technical explanations and the senior vice president for strategic conclusions, was a great success. The Goldman Senior Partner, recognizing the "excellency" of our model, proposed that I remain in charge of "all the number".

I value this experience because I gained respect from the senior executives at all three firms. But most of all, although one of the most junior banker, I was able to inspire a cohesive spirit to our team in pursuing our goal to produce a high quality presentation.

Learning to Surf

My move to Los Angeles last August represented not only a great professional challenge—to work with only two senior bankers and cover all California financial institutions—but also a personal opportunity, a chance to broaden my horizons. I grew up in Paris and lived in the capital for 21 years before moving to New York; I definitely was a city girl! Los Angeles demanded however that I adapted to a whole different world, where sport rather than opera rhythms the season. I knew that my first year in the Los Angeles office would be extremely busy due to the small size of my group. In fact I averaged 90 hours of work per week that year. To keep my sanity and maintain a good spirit, I resolved to try and learn a sport that had always fascinated me: surfing. Thus I bought a brand new wetsuit and longboard and started the experience bright and early on a sunny Saturday afternoon under the merciless scrutiny of the local surfers, all males, who did not hide their contempt for my pale skin and weak arms so typical of investment banking Corporate Analysts. Surfing seemed at first an impossible mission: my board always mysteriously rebounded on my head, while the waves would break exactly where I was paddling. At work, there was an explosion of laughter when I proudly exposed my (only) personal project: why, a twenty-six year old Parisian, surfing? This had to be French humor! I resolved however to practice every weekend before coming into the office. Last summer, I finally stood up on my board and rode the wave to the beach. It was one of the most exhilarating moments of my life and although I still surf regularly, nothing matches my first wave nor the pride that I felt. Because I received little help and encouragement but prevailed, I cherish this experience which was actually a tremendous confidence builder.

Comments

The writer demonstrates a nice balance between her professional and her personal achievements. Her first accomplishment shows the essayist to be a savvy business professional and highlights her good political sense, dedication, and technical skill. The second accomplishment rounds out the image by painting a picture of a young, healthy, active woman willing to take risks and learn new skills at the expense of laughter and embarrassment. The latter may have been a personal achievement, but these translate into very lucrative professional skills as well.

ESSAY 13: Harvard, entrepreneur, hockey player

Describe your three most substantial accomplishments, and explain why you view them as such.

I believe the following three accomplishments illustrates different personal qualities that are integral in a successful contributor to Harvard Business School.

1) Initiative/Entrepreneurship

During the summer before my senior year, I founded and managed a company that employed five people and grossed twenty thousand dollars. I was faced with a very difficult employment environment, and had to turn down several unpaid internships in the financial arena because I was paying the majority of my tuition. With no capital and no practical experience, I decided to start my own company. I spent several days researching the options and discussing possibilities. I identified the fundamental characteristics that my business had to possess to compete successfully and profitably. It was mandatory that there be minimal start up expenses or working capital needs. I needed to compete in a historically overpriced channel of distribution, so that a company with no economy of scale could survive. I wanted a strong reliance on marketing, but on marketing a service more than a product. Taking all of this into consideration, I created Collegiate Window Washing. I spent the first two weeks pounding the pavement, planning to build a client backlog to last one month, assuming that references and further marketing would take over from there. I purchased the necessary equipment, and hired two friends from college and three high school students. I assembled three teams that would work separately, each completing one to two houses per day. I personally handled the payroll, scheduling, marketing, and expense management. The business was very successful, and the experience was especially satisfying. Clearly, the skills I developed from running a business were beneficial, but the initiative and entrepreneurial effort were the most important things I took from that summer.

2) Perseverance

In my senior year at Harvard, I led our ECAC champion hockey team in points, becoming the first player to ever begin his career on the J.V. team and finish as the varsity's leading scorer. The three men who led our team in scoring in my first three years in the program were amazingly talented and heavily recruited. They were essential players even in their freshman seasons. They have since spent time playing in the NHL. By contrast, I was not heavily recruited, and spent very little time with the varsity during my freshman year. If you had asked any diehard Harvard hockey fan who I was after my freshman season, they would not have had a clue. Considering that very few players ever move from the J.V. to the varsity, I was terribly discouraged following that first season. My two older brothers had played for Harvard almost twenty years before, and my lifelong goal had been to be the third. I turned down acceptances from Yale, Princeton, and Harvard to take a post-graduate year at Hotchkiss in the hopes that I would mature academically and athletically, and make a meaningful contribution during my four years in Cambridge. After my freshman season, that looked very unlikely.

However, there was no way that I was going to abandon such an important part of my life without a concerted effort. I spent that summer, and the two following it, working fifty to sixty hours a week in construction, investment banking, and managing my own company, coupled with daily workouts that usually lasted three to four hours. I turned down several offers for enjoyable summers with my friends or teammates in Nantucket or driving across the country. I couldn't afford to, because my freshman year had shown me that talent alone wasn't enough to allow me to reach the goal I had set for myself. It is not necessary to detail each game during my four years, but simply to note the progression from borderline player to starter. If you asked that same Harvard fan today who led the Harvard team in scoring in that year, he'd probably guess five names before mine, especially since I didn't continue on to play professionally, as several of my teammates did. I had offers to play both in the U.S. and in Europe, but I decided to give up hockey and pursue a career in business. My goal in life, athletically, was to be a meaningful contributor to the Harvard team. Am I proud that I lead the team in scoring that year? Sure. But the perseverance and dedication that it took to get there are far more important to me.

3) Time Management/Breadth of Experience

I paid for the majority of my college education, while achieving Dean's List every semester, spent forty hours each week participating in a Division 1 athletic program, worked ten to fifteen hours each week to help defray tuition costs, and also maintained a balanced social life. I welcomed the opportunity to take on the majority of the tuition burden, but unfortunately the income I generated each summer was not sufficient. It became necessary for me to work two or three shifts each week on top of an already mentally and physically draining schedule. To illustrate a typical day:

8:00–8:30	Breakfast
8:30–12:00	3 Lectures
12:00–12:30	Lunch
12:30–2:00	Lab, Section, or Study
2:00–6:00	Practice, Work out
6:00–6:30	Dinner
6:30–10:00	Job
10:00–12:00	Study, Friends

Keep in mind that this is only a typical day. Every other weekend during the season (the longest of any sport, beginning September 30 and ending April 1), the hockey team would go on road trips, leaving Cambridge at 5 P.M. on Thursday and returning early Sunday morning. The class time that I had missed, and the study time lost had to be crammed into a shortened week. During exam periods or midterms, there was never enough time in the day, as the practices didn't cease and the tuition bills didn't go away. This also doesn't account for the level of emotional and mental stress that accompanies trying to excel in one of the finest academic settings in the country, while also competing for a perennial national power in college athletics. I am proud not of any one accomplishment, academic or athletic, during my college years, but that I was able, through constant time management and diligence, to excel in several areas of campus life. Most importantly, I took a mature step towards financial independence in funding the majority of my Harvard tuition.

Comments

All three of these illustrations are wonderful. The first two are completely independent from one another and show two very different sides of this applicant. The third shows what he had to do to balance these different facets—a fact that an admissions officer could easily overlook. Many applicants would not have seen the opportunity inherent in listing this last achievement. In doing so, the essayist elevates the first two accomplishments to new levels, leaving the reader feeling positive about the applicant.

ESSAY 14: Michigan, Teach For America

Describe your achievements within the last five years that are good indicators of your potential for a successful management career and why you view them as such.

Teaching as a Teach For America corps member

Upon graduating from college, I joined Teach For America to teach for two years in one of our nation's most under-resourced public schools. During my teaching assignment in Baton Rouge, I worked with children who were forced to cope daily with shocking violence and squalor. One of my students had to crawl across his kitchen floor at night to avoid bullets that ripped through his windows; a girl in my class was sexually abused by her father; and another student found his father shot to death on his front doorstep. To motivate these students, I had to be creative despite my very limited resources. I initiated a support group for the most at-risk children in our school, and I reached beyond the four walls of my classroom by involving parents and relating my lessons to my students' everyday lives. In the end, I saw my efforts pay off, as all thirty of my students (some starting at pre-kindergarten reading and math levels) finished the year at their appropriate grade level, having passed a statewide standardized test. More importantly, though, my students left my class excited about learning and inquisitive about the world around them.

Raising funds for Teach For America

A year and a half ago, Wendy Kopp, the founder and president of Teach For America, tapped me to become the non-profit organization's Director of National Development. With no fundraising experience, I rose to the challenge of raising $2.9 million annually. Not only have I accomplished this seemingly formidable task, but I have also succeeded in diversifying our funding base. Since I first became Director of National Development, we have staged TFA's first marketing partnerships with corporations like the American Automobile Association and Seagrams. We have also raised over $100,000 in pro bono donations, held our first public events, and received $4 million from our first federal grants. In engineering these initiatives, I have learned about the art of fundraising and I have also had the pleasure of helping Teach For America grow from a fledgling start-up organization into a long-lasting stable institution.

I am confident that as I enter my next career phase of launching my own non-profit organization, I will be able to manage its program and staff successfully. To lead my third grade class and the Teach For America organization, I have had to motivate individuals with many different personalities, interests and backgrounds. In addition to my long and dedicated work weeks, I have been an active volunteer within my community. Currently, I chair an environmental education organization for inner-city children, and also serve in a high school mentoring program. Both inside and outside of work, I have cooperated with peers, supervisors, mentors, and people whom I have managed along the way. Through all of this, I have come to realize that my initiative, determination, sense of humor, and continual striving for excellence enable me to overcome what seem even the greatest of challenges.

Comments

This concise essay shows a personal side but does so within the context of two professional achievements. The nature of the writer's profession is itself very personal, which makes demonstrating her qualities as a caring individual involved in the community easier to do. She manages to fit some quite vivid descriptions into a short space. The essayist also finishes each accomplishment with detailed proofs of her success, "All thirty of my students finished the year at their appropriate grade level," and "We have raised over $100,000 in pro bono donations . . . and received $4 million from our first federal grants." Accountability and proof in numbers are both very important in the business world and are always extremely effective in essays.

CHAPTER 9

Leadership
Abilities

- This question offers another opportunity for engaging storytelling.
- Let the focus of the story demonstrate your leadership skills.
- Experiences outside of work can be equally meaningful.

This question is similar to the accomplishment question. You can employ similar tactics to answer it. Choose situations that are real and meaningful to you, not what you think will impress the committee the most. Do not limit yourself to using situations from only your career, especially if the question asks you to give more than one example.

This question shares common ground, surprisingly, with the ethical dilemma question because ethical dilemmas often call on leadership abilities for resolution. Keep this in the back of your mind so you can strategize if one of your applications asks both questions. On the other hand, be careful not to bring unnecessary attention to questionable situations when not absolutely necessary. Ethical dilemma questions are notoriously difficult; this question does not have to be.

ESSAY 15: Harvard, hockey player
Describe a situation that tested your leadership skills. How did you manage the situation?

The Lead-In:
- Championship Game, Great Lakes Invitational Tournament
- Sellout crowd of 19,000, National T.V. audience
- Harvard 1 Michigan 1, late in the final period.
I carried the puck up the left wing and couldn't find a teammate as I reached the offensive zone. It was late in the shift, so I dumped the

puck into the far corner, retreated to the bench, and was replaced by the freshman left wing on the second line. Moments later, Michigan transitioned nicely, leaving our three forwards caught in the offensive zone. Their initial rush was stopped, but the rebound spun out to their trailing wing, the freshman's responsibility. The Michigan player scored, and the goal gave them the championship, a devastating blow as we all felt we had outplayed them and should be bringing the trophy back to Cambridge.

The Situation:

We undressed slowly in the locker room until the coach entered and all activity stopped. He was understandably upset at the loss and the defensive breakdown that had cost us the title. He berated us for our lack of effort and discipline. He then moved to a theme that I hadn't heard before, challenging the senior class for their lack of leadership. Already upset, I was thoroughly unprepared for what was next. Wheeling around quickly, he faced me and said, "I can't believe that we have a senior, a guy who's supposed to be a leader, who's so selfish that rather than dumping the puck in the zone late in the game when he's tired, decides to be the hero. He wants to score the big goal and get the glory, but instead he gets caught and his man beats him back up the ice to score the winner. That play cost us the game, that's the kind of thing I'm talking about. One guy's selfishness can cost us a game."

The Test:

I was stunned and demoralized. In the heat of the moment, he hadn't noticed that I had done the unselfish thing, and was actually sitting on the bench right in front of him when the winning goal was scored. Unfortunately, there were only two people in the room that knew I was not at fault, so after his tirade the other 22 players now believed that I had let the team down. With a team that was as close as we were, and one in which I was supposed to be a leader, there was no greater sin. In the moments after his accusation, I wrestled with feelings of anger, sadness, and confusion. My immediate reaction was to respond, I thought I would explode if I didn't defend myself. As I looked across at the freshman, he stared blankly at me with tears in his eyes. I stared directly at the coach, a full 5 seconds passed, and he walked away, over to console our goalie. The opportunity for redemption in the eyes of my teammates had passed. However, the situation was not over, and neither was the opportunity to absolve myself. We returned to Cambridge, and had two days off before resuming practice. I was informed shortly before taking the ice that I had been moved from the first line to the fourth line, effective immediately. The practice was a blur, as I watched the progress I had made from J.V. player to major contributor evaporate in a case of mistaken identity.

Playing hockey at Harvard had been a lifelong dream, born on freezing nights in Watson Rink 15 years earlier watching my two oldest brothers play for the Crimson. The dream was quickly turning into a nightmare, as I knew the coach's opinion of me had been altered. I spent the next two days considering the proper course I should take to correct the mistake. We had a game tape right in the locker room. I could tell the Captain, who was one of my best friends. I could tell the assistant coach. Or I could confront the coach myself. I had a hundred opportunities over the next few days to clear my name. With each passing day, it was apparent that I wouldn't do it. It's been three years, and I still haven't. Why?

The Decision:

It would not have been difficult, in a practical sense, to let the coach know that I had not been at fault, that the freshman was the one caught up ice, but it was simply a physical mistake, and not an act of selfishness on his part. It was possible that no one would really be hurt by my disclosure. I had several days to think about the situation and decided against speaking up for a multitude of reasons, some of which aren't easily explainable. For me to absolve myself, I would have had to compromise a teammates' standing. With any teammate, I would have had a tough time doing it. There are several ideals in a group setting more important than personal satisfaction. Loyalty, Teamwork, Character. Most importantly, how could I have called myself a leader if I had acted any other way? Moreover, the fact that the other player was this particular freshman precluded me from even considering clearing my name. He was me, 3 years earlier. Young for his class, somewhat in awe of his surroundings, and clinging to a spot on the varsity. I was at the end of my career and fully deserved playing time. I had earned it, improving with each season. If I was to clear my name and compromise his, likely robbing him of the opportunity that I had capitalized on three years earlier, what would I have gained? The only thing I had to gain from reversing the situation was personal redemption. I decided there were other ways to achieve that. I worked diligently in practice and slowly moved back up the ladder to my original slot. The freshman also improved consistently, and was one of our steadier players by season's end.

Leadership is not appointed, it is earned. It does not have to be vocal, but must be constant. It is most certainly not convenient, but it is most definitely necessary. Leadership is often not clear in times of success, but is magnified in times of challenge. Leaders must often choose a course of action that is most beneficial to the group that he or she represents, regardless of the personal impact. Our team went on to capture the ECAC championship, a feat that we had not accomplished the previous two years with far more talented teams. There were several situations over the 30 game season where I thought our young team might falter, but the six seniors would not allow this to happen. I don't know how many times each one of them chose to sacrifice for the good of the team, and I'm positive that none of them had any idea about the incident in Michigan or the decision I made. Leadership does not need to be obvious or heroic or monumental. It only needs to be consistent and uncompromising.

Comments

This applicant is a wonderful writer and makes great use of the storytelling technique. He definitely draws the reader in, and the conclusions he makes in the last paragraph are heartfelt and meaningful. Without the story, the points he made in his conclusion would have sounded posed, didactic, or stilted. Without the elucidation, the story might have made the writer's decision to remain silent seem less like leadership and more like avoidance or failure to confront a situation.

ESSAY 16: Anderson, engineer

Discuss two situations in the past four years where you have taken an active leadership role. How do these events demonstrate your managerial potential?

Wellwork Action Team

After working for nearly a year as a production engineer, one morning I experienced a kind of epiphany. I realized that our profit center had effectively gained manpower and resources in the form of increased attention from vendors with whom we had recently formed strategic alliances. By improving communication between these vendors as well as between our profit center and these companies, I envisioned a unified approach that could improve and expedite our production operations. With the encouragement of the operations superintendent, I arranged a brainstorming session for supervisory level personnel from our operations staff and our new alliance partner's companies. From that session, a "Wellwork Action Team" was created with the specific purpose of improving and streamlining our operations procedures in order to reduce the cost of increase the quality of our projects in the field.

After being chosen facilitator for our Wellwork Action Team, I set for myself two personal goals: first, to maintain enthusiasm among team members and second, to implement the ideas and concepts brought forth by our team into our everyday procedures. To ensure continued involvement, I first convinced myself that the potential benefits that might be gained from having this team merited the time and energy of its participants. Next, I personally committed myself to the project and firmly discussed my commitment with each of team members. Third, I led the team in drafting a mission statement and clearly defining our goals. We identified measurements by which we could evaluate our progress. Finally, I promised the team members that we would keep meetings to a minimum and re-evaluate the usefulness of our team in eight weeks.

Within the span of a few months, our Wellwork Action Team has successfully increased efficiency in our oil pumps, reduced electrical costs by 6 percent, and nearly doubled the production of three oil wells. As our team continues to evolve, we envision reducing our wellwork budget from $5.0 million/year to $4.6 million/year while maintaining oil production and reducing operating expenses. Our current challenges include overcoming conflicts in the schedules of our team members and providing for long-term oil recovery as well as short-term cost reduction.

Applying New Technologies

When most people envision an oil well, they picture ten-foot-high rod pumping units, the kind common to Los Angeles and West Texas because of their durability, availability, and efficiency. With 300 wells on a mere 10 acre island, however, these units are impractical for our use; a less efficient, higher cost and lower-profile type of centrifugal pump is employed by our company. Recently, a small L.A. firm invented a new method of using common rod-type pumps without the bulky surface equipment. This marriage of new technology with old rod-style pumping appeared to have significant potential for reducing costs on our island. Although I do not normally design our pumping equipment, I assumed active project leadership when deciding to install the first unit and apply the new technology.

Because our operations personnel and vendor partners were unaccustomed to handling hundreds of 30-foot long rods and putting them into use, I met with the inventor of the new subsurface equipment and two related vendors who would supply the rods. Rather than provide specifications to each vendor for a bid as is customary, I chose one vendor from the onset and entrusted him with the project. I assigned him to work with the inventor of the new equipment and asked them to together devise a low cost, high quality engineering design for us. In doing so, the possibility existed for them to overdesign and overprice the equipment, reducing efficiency and thus defeating our purpose. Nevertheless, a tremendous upside potential existed in allowing the vendors to harmonize their efforts and experience. I hoped to receive a superior product born from the sweat equity of their two companies.

My strategy was tested last November when two units were installed. They have operated without failure since installation and have reduced operating costs by 38 percent on those wells. In this instance, my management challenge was to delegate non-traditional responsibilities to our vendors. I feel that this experience has improved our business process and taken us further down the path towards mutually beneficial business relationships with our vendors. I will continue to work in this manner, keeping a careful eye out for the abuse potential created when allowing a vendor to design and price their own equipment for our applications.

Comments

These two examples have several positive qualities. First, they are concise and well structured. Second, although both situations come from the professional sphere, they balance well with each other. One focuses more on office policy and stresses the applicant's ability to see the big picture in management. The other deals with an in-the-field, hands-on engineering solution and stresses his inventiveness, attention to detail, and technological skills. Third, these examples stress unique background—not many business school applicants would understand how to design oil pumping equipment. They show that he is not afraid to get his hands dirty. Finally, the essayist gives very detailed proof of tangible results.

Essay 17: Anderson, consulting analyst

Discuss two situations in the past four years where you have taken an active leadership role. How do these events demonstrate your managerial potential?

While I have had many opportunities to serve in the capacity of a leader in both my personal and professional lives, there are two occasions that I feel clearly demonstrate my managerial potential. During my first few months as an analyst for a large consulting firm, I was participating on a study with an extremely tight time-frame. It was the afternoon before the deadline and my project team and I were supposed to present the results of our cost benchmarking study to the client hospital the following morning. As we were reviewing the materials for the presentation, I noticed that one of the calculations on which we based our primary analysis was incorrect. As a result of the miscalculation, the financial savings that the client hospital would realize by altering its Nursing department skill mix was grossly misstated. After I informed the senior project manager of the mistake, he told our project team to ignore it. As his reasons, he stated that the project was not "worth that much" and that the client would never discover the mistake.

Even though I felt unprepared to supervise the rebuilding of the analysis, I realized the gravity of the situation and decided to take the lead. Not only did the client hospital's viability depend on the accuracy of our work, but my company's reputation could be in jeopardy as well. After explaining the situation to my teammates, I asked for volunteers who felt, as I did, that the problem should be fixed prior to the presentation, and who were willing to work all night to correct it. I took the lead in dividing up the required tasks among the remaining team members so that the work would be completed in an efficient and timely manner. Furthermore, I monitored each person's progress throughout the night, answering technical questions to the best of my ability and verifying that the analysis was re-run correctly. The next morning our project team was able to present accurate findings of which we could be proud.

Another significant leadership experience occurred shortly after my promotion to Senior Analyst at the consulting firm. While managing a client engagement is usually not a responsibility of analysts at any level, I was eager to broaden my role at the company. I volunteered to lead a team of analysts on a critical study, in which our client hospital system was entering into negotiations to be acquired by a large West-Coast based hospital chain. I was the primary client contact, working directly with the administrators at the hospital to design analyses examining their hospitals' profitability, quality of care, and efficiency of delivery. I was also called to lead frequent meetings and conference calls with top executives from the hospital to explain our methodologies and research findings. Furthermore, I managed a team of junior business analysts, computer analysts, programmers, graphics artists, and administrative support staff throughout the duration of the lengthy project.

I feel that my demonstrated leadership during these two events is an excellent indicator of my managerial potential. In both situations, I was required to supervise and coordinate teams of diverse staff members, from administrative support personnel to my analyst peers. This ability will prove essential in a management career considering the dominance of team settings in today's global business environment. In addition, I delegated tasks efficiently under tight deadlines, all of which were met. I feel that this accomplishment manifests two key management aptitudes, organizational skills and the ability to quickly prioritize tasks. Furthermore, I never hesitated to work long hours, hand-in-hand with those I managed. I intend to be a business leader that builds trust and respect in my team and models their benefits by example.

Also indicative of my managerial potential is my demonstrated ability to make spontaneous decisions and to instinctively answer difficult questions. Even though I had only been with the consulting firm for a few months, as I led the team to revise the analysis in the first example, I drew on my past experiences to make educated guesses in the face of

ESSAYS THAT WILL GET YOU INTO BUSINESS SCHOOL

uncertainties. As a leader, I also displayed confidence when the team encountered obstacles. It was essential to both projects' success to have a leader that never gave up looking for solutions to the often overwhelming dilemmas we encountered.

Lastly, in these two leadership roles, I was required to manage not only people, but also entire processes. From designing the analyses, to coordinating the analysts, to effectively managing the clients expectations, to circumventing potential problems, I had to be a true leader in that all aspects of the study were my responsibility. I look forward to participating in a challenging M.B.A. program, through which I will be able to build on the leadership skills I have already gained, as I further develop my management techniques.

Comments

The first situation this applicant mentions could have answered an ethical dilemma question. It is not always wise to call attention to a questionable situation if you are not directly asked to do so. Although she does demonstrate leadership with this example, the writer also acted against the wishes of the senior project manager, which could raise a red flag. The second example is a better one, though not as thought provoking. She could have made her conclusion (which spans three paragraphs) more concise and to the point.

ESSAY 18: Wharton WEMBA

Describe the most significant way, either in or out of your job, in which you have demonstrated leadership.

One of the most unique times I remember leading was also one of the most unexpected. It was not planned that I led this group, nor did anyone expect that the group needed leading. It was a Sunday morning when I was 18 years old. It was sometime in December, although I don't remember the exact date. I was still in college and my mother and a few friends from the entertainment industry had gotten together and decided to gather some donated items (clothes, toys, even cigarettes and dog food) to give to the less fortunate people in the downtown Los Angeles area. She asked me to help and I said sure, thinking it a worthy cause.

People donated much more than we expected. And when the day came to give out the goods, we ended up with enough stuff to fill a very large moving truck. So off we went—me, my mother and 10 others, on our way to help out the homeless. At about 7:00 A.M. or so, we arrived at our destination—an empty street corner in the lower section of downtown LA. There were a few people sleeping in boxes scattered around the area but by in large, it was empty. We opened the back of the truck and started approaching the people sleeping in the street, asking them if we could help them a little with some of our donations. It began slowly with people walking up to the back of the truck asking for something. Within 30 minutes, there must have been 100 or more people in a crowd around the back of the truck—homeless people clamoring in almost a violent mob, pushing and shoving, yelling, fighting for the clothes or cigarettes, jumping in the truck and overwhelming all of us.

At some point I saw an old man get pushed to the ground by a teenager who grabbed something off the truck. We had no control and what started out as a good spirited mission, turned into a hateful morning. It was at that moment, when everything was going out of control, that I made a decision. I didn't think about doing it, it just happened. I grabbed a couple of the bigger guys from our group, closed the back of the truck, got our group together and left. We left an angry mob without accomplishing anything. No goodwill, no help, no good feelings—nothing.

I remember feeling desensitized by their disrespect for what we were doing. I was thinking to myself, "How could they? They don't deserve our kindness." I was determined to drive the truck to the dump and get rid of everything we had. I wasn't going to help them if they couldn't behave like civilized people.

I don't remember what happened next, maybe someone said something in our group, but I suddenly realized that I was being selfish. These people didn't have anything. Many of the homeless people that I had just seen had been on the street for years. Who was I to impose my ideas on them or to judge them? We came to help and we should carry out our mission. I had the team pull over and we got out and talked. I talked about how we were here to help and how we had to try to feel what they were feeling. We had a long and heated discussion and finally came up with an answer. We parked the truck along a side street and put a few items in each team member's car. Then each car went around and stopped whenever they saw someone on the street that could use a hand, offered something from the back of the car and went on. When they were done they came back to the truck and reloaded. No large truck in sight, no angry mob, no old man getting trampled, no one afraid that they would not get their share. We went about doing this the entire day and by the time sunset came, most of the items had been given away.

It took me many years to understand that I became a leader that day and that my leadership changed the outcome of what would have otherwise been a very sad situation. I didn't plan to be the leader. My leadership came from my basic instincts and the fact that I was willing to look at things from a different perspective. Leadership has always been a difficult trait for me to categorize. It seems that some individuals lead by doing what they think is right and having others follow, while others focus on leading a group simply for leadership's sake. I have always been able to lead when I sense a true need and others seem to always follow. The lesson I learned that day took me many years to understand, but looking back across time I realize it was one of the first and most important times that I stepped outside myself to lead and make a difference.

Comments

Although the story that the essayist tells makes the essay interesting, the leadership qualities that are demonstrated are questionable. His/her actions seem rash and unpredictable—at one moment closing the truck and leaving an angry mob, and then for no apparent reason, stopping the truck and prompting everyone to change direction. The essayist comes off as wildly emotional and seems to delegate tasks without much thought about the consequences. Luckily, none of these volunteers were harmed after approaching people on the street, who were unquestionably in need but who (as a group) have a high rate of mental illness and/or substance abuse and whose reactions were unpredictable.

A good lesson to be learned from this example is to choose a scenario that doesn't just document a leadership event, but one that demonstrates solid leadership ability and good decision making skills. The outcome of the event is not as important as the leadership qualities it proves.

CHAPTER 10

Hobbies and Extracurriculars

- This type of question demands a personal approach.
- It is imperative to showcase your interests outside of academics and your career.
- Prove that you are interesting and well rounded.

This question offers a prime opportunity to differentiate yourself by presenting a vivid description of your life outside of work. Business schools are interested in balanced, likable applicants. Your professional life is only part of an interrelated whole. Business schools expect you to demonstrate the same level of dedication and passion in outside activities as you do in business. They are also well aware that many of the best business-related ideas occur when people are not at work, so what you do out of the office has a measurable impact on what you can do on the job. Besides, funny, offbeat, interesting people make work, school, and essays more exciting. Communicate feelings of passion, commitment, and devotion. Wherever possible, demonstrate the leadership abilities you have developed in these activities.

ESSAY 19: Wharton, tutor
What one nonprofessional activity do you find most inspirational and why? (Wharton)

A little over two years ago I began tutoring high school students in several types of mathematics, including preparation for the S.A.T. Test. While I did this initially to earn money, I have continued to tutor (often pro bono) because I enjoy the material and the contact with the students.

99

I have always enjoyed math tremendously. I can remember riding in a car for long distances as a child and continuously calculating average speeds and percentages of distances covered as we traveled. In college I took upper division math classes such as Real Analysis and Game Theory (and placed near the top of the curve) though they were not required for my major. All this time spent playing with math has left me with a deep understanding of the way numbers work and the many ways in which problems can be solved.

When I first began tutoring I was stunned to find that most of the kids I worked with, although very bright, not only lacked the ability to solve complex problems, they were very uncomfortable with some of the basic principles of math. This discomfort led to fear and avoidance, and the avoidance led to more discomfort. A vicious cycle began. Instead of seeing math as a beautiful system in which arithmetic, algebra and geometry all worked together to allow one to solve problems, they saw it as a bunch of jumbled rules which made little sense that they were forced to memorize.

As a tutor, I found that it was important when starting with a new student to find out where his/her discomfort with math began. Often, this meant going back several years in their education to explain important basic concepts. For some students, fractions and decimals were the point at which math stopped making sense. For many others, it was the introduction of letters to represent numbers in algebra. Some students found that identifying their weaknesses was an embarrassing process. I explained to them that it was not their fault. Everyone comes to understand new concepts in math in a slightly different way, and the problem was that no teacher had taken the time to explain their "problem area" in a way which would make sense to them. Since math was a system, once they missed out on that one building block, it was not surprising that the rest of it did not make sense. Our mission together would be to find the way in which the system worked for them.

Once we had identified the initial "problem area," I would spend a lot of time getting the student to play with questions in that area from a lot of different perspectives. For example, if fractions were the problem, then I would create games to get the student to think of fractions in terms of division, ratios, decimals or other equivalent systems. This would often be a fairly unstructured process, as I wanted to see how the student's mind worked and keep them from feeling any anxiety. Usually it did not take long for the concepts to start becoming clear to the student, as he/she played with the numbers in the absence of the pressure of school. My goal was to not just white wash over a students weaknesses with a few rules which would be quickly forgotten, but to help them develop an understanding and an appreciation for the underlying principles.

I found this process to be very satisfying for both myself and the young men and women that I taught. It was a wonderful feeling to have a student laugh out loud with relief as a principle which had been unclear and causing anxiety for years suddenly made sense. Once these old "problem areas" were cleared up it was usually quite simple to make clear the subjects that they were working on at the time, especially since I already had an understanding of how they were best able to understand new concepts. Again, I found it important to get the student to play with the new material and look at it in several ways so as to develop a true understanding of the material.

I was quite successful as a tutor. One young man increased his Math S.A.T. by 150 points. Another student improved so dramatically in geometry, her test scores jumped from about 55 percent to over 90 percent, that her teacher kept her after class and asked if she was cheating. Although most of my students did not improve this dramatically, I walked away from every lesson that I gave feeling that I had helped someone understand and enjoy math. I hope to be able to continue teaching, if only for a few hours a week, for the rest of my life.

Comments

This essay shows that this applicant is dedicated not just to helping people, but to academics, learning, and math. His tutoring does not make us believe his sincerity; the thoughtfulness and detail with which he describes it do. He has put obvious time into developing an effective method of teaching. The writer shows that he is result-oriented by measuring his success in terms of real numbers and percentage increases. Someone who applies such standards of accountability to his extracurricular life is sure to bring the same standards to school and business.

ESSAY 20: Kellogg, runner

For fun I . . .

Another hectic day at the office has left me a little on edge. As I travel home through the subterranean passages of the subway, I can feel the tension radiating off me in waves. When I reach my apartment, I quickly exchange my suit and tie for shorts and a tank top. I do a couple of stretching exercises, slip on my Pumas, grab my Walkman (already loaded with my favorite Sonic Youth tape), and I go.

Less than one hour later, my breath escapes my lungs in short gasps, I can feel my heart pounding in my chest to the rhythm of my shoes hitting the pavement; and although it's a brisk thirty-eight degrees outside, sweat races down my face. As I approach the end of my route down Washington Square's brownstone-lined streets, I explode into a mad sprint. I dart past other runners and even some of the slower cyclists and roller-bladers as I complete the last one hundred yards of my personal six-mile race.

I click my stop-watch when I pass the slender tree that marks my imaginary finish line, and I shift down into a medium-paced stagger. I raise my wrist to check out today's time. The L.C.D. numbers read 45:07.43. I quickly calculate that I was running at a seven-and-a-half-minute mile pace. Good, but I can do better. I smile, because that's what I always say to myself, whether I've just completed a run or a presentation. Because I know that I'm my own toughest competitor, and I'll always have to run a little bit faster if I want to keep up.

Comments

Beauty is in simplicity—even where admissions are concerned. The writer avoids belaboring the reader with lengthy rhetoric explaining why his activity makes him a better person and candidate, which spells relief for a tired admissions officer. This essay is a perfect example of showing, not telling. Compare this with the next essay, which approaches a similar subject more typically.

ESSAY 21: Wharton, windsurfer
What one nonprofessional activity do you find most inspirational and why?

In reflecting upon the activities that I pursue outside of work, I find that the time I spend windsurfing in Hong Kong is not only among the most enjoyable, but it is also the activity that most inspires me. Upon moving to Hong Kong eighteen months ago, I decided to resume my practice of windsurfing, a sport I was forced to abandon while living in New York city. Despite a busy schedule and waters that are anything but crystal clear, I have managed to spend a few hours a month pursuing this activity. Apart from the incredible physical experience, I have learned to appreciate the time I spend windsurfing because of the sense of accomplishment, freedom, and challenge that it offers. The inspiration that I obtain from windsurfing causes me to approach both my professional and personal activities with a renewed sense of purpose and commitment.

My enjoyment of windsurfing results partly from the advances that I have made in mastering the technical aspects of this sport since my first expedition approximately ten years ago. Windsurfing is a fairly difficult sport that requires both a knowledge of sailing skills as well as physical strength and balance. Like many beginners, my first attempts at windsurfing ended in clear failure. To this day, I distinctly remember the distraught feeling of floating down the bank of the Potomac River because I did not know how to sail against the wind! My ensuing experiences usually ended with similar results until I finally decided to take a two-day training course. Armed with the fundamentals of sailing, I tackled the sport anew and ever so slowly progressed to being able to sail both with and against the wind. Over the past eighteen months, I have taken advantage of Hong Kong's many beaches to advance my skills and knowledge to the point where I have become a fairly accomplished windsurfer. Although the development of my technical skills and ability over the past ten years has been challenging and sometimes painful (literally), I can look back on this as an experience where I demonstrated great dedication and commitment to achieve a personal goal.

I also love windsurfing because, more than any other activity, it allows me to escape the pressure and stress of my professional responsibilities by providing me with a sense of freedom and abandon. Investment banking is generally recognized for its heavy workload and intense environment. Combined with frequent travel and a necessity to operate across different time zones, my position requires that I dedicate most of my time to professional activities. As a result, I value my personal time highly and greatly anticipate those few hours in the week when I can escape the professional responsibilities placed upon me. Windsurfing provides just such an opportunity because it forces me to concentrate on only those elements that influence my direction and speed—the wind, water, sail, and my body. When I am on the water, I forget about all of my concerns and simply enjoy the freedom and tranquillity that results from being alone with nature. This feeling is magnified by the solitude and abandon that I experience, as I am dependent upon my own abilities to direct my craft. As a result, I find the few hours I spend windsurfing result in greater professional productivity by reducing my stress level and giving me renewed energy and focus.

Despite the improvement in my windsurfing skills, I continue to be fascinated with the sport because it offers constant challenge for me to test my abilities against the forces of nature. When I first started windsurfing, the challenge was simply to stand on the board and hold on to the sail for a few minutes before a gust of wind pushed me into the water. As I progressed, the challenge became one of learning how to manipulate the wind to suit my own objectives. Along the way, I learned that regardless of how far my technical skills and knowledge advanced, the forces of nature would continue to present me with situations and challenges that I was unprepared for and unable to control. Although the result of these experiences was usually a tumble into the water, the opportunity to test myself in challenging situations and learn from them is one of the aspects of windsurfing that I most enjoy. In learning how to deal with the natural elements, I have found that the same forces that cause me to move rapidly across the water can also quickly change, resulting in a high-speed crash with painful consequences. The constant challenge that results from attempting to control these natural forces with my own ability is an inspiring experience.

I believe that my love of windsurfing, and the inspiration that I receive from this sport, is partially due to the fact that this activity is so very different from my professional endeavours. Unlike investment banking where multiple objectives and constraints come into play, windsurfing is essentially a very basic activity where the objective is to control natural forces through the use of a sail and board to suit one's own goal. Operating by myself with no guidance or supervision, responsibility for success or failure is easy to assign while the only reward I seek is the enjoyment of my own efforts. Although I enjoy the challenges and rewards of working in a team-oriented environment such as investment banking, windsurfing offers inspiration on a personal level because it allows me to escape to a more natural environment where the risks are straightforward and the rewards a result of my skills and actions.

Comments

Compare this with the last essay (written by the runner) to see a similar subject approached in a completely different way. This approach is more typical and preferable unless the applicant is a confident and accomplished writer. This applicant does not let the activity stand by itself—he explains why he finds it worthwhile and what he has learned from it. In short, this essay accomplishes what it should. It accurately answers the question and shows the candidate to be a balanced and well-rounded individual.

ESSAY 22: Kellogg, entertainer
Outside of work, I most enjoy . . .

"It's in my blood, it's in my veins, I am the ghost who entertains."

—Peter Weiss, *Wie dem Herrn Mockinpott das Leiden ausgetrieben wird*

Entertaining an audience requires three ingredients: the entertainer himself; the medium he uses to entertain; a receptive audience. To take on the role of the entertainer, that certainly is the activity I enjoy most besides work, and I do it in three different contexts, defined by medium used and audience addressed.

The first context, and the one occurring by far the most frequently, is simple conversation. Whenever the situation allows, I let my mind jump around the topic at hand and explore all kinds of strange, and often funny, associations. As soon as I have found something, I let my partners know, and very often it makes them laugh; more than once this playful thinking around the problem has led to a completely new and useful approach. My colleagues find me extraordinarily quickwitted and jovial and equipped with an "unconditional sense of humour"—that is the kind of feedback I get in (Big Consulting Company), group dynamics seminars.

The second context requires much more preparation: It starts with a journey to some far-away destination—usually accompanied by one or more close friends. On location I collect material: shooting videos (mainly for scenes involving movement) and taking slides (mainly for landscapes and snapshots) describing the trip. When I get home, I take the very best slides and the best video footage and combine the whole into a Multimedia, integrated slide/videoshow. I have developed my very own style for that, working with two screens which at times use their respective medium to show the same object, at times show related, but not identical content, and at times simply present a straightforward copy of the other screen. This gives me a powerful tool to put the spectator's mind into different states of activity and convey all kinds of messages.

To prepare such a show completely, with all picture and sound effects and selection of the right music, is an immensely complex task. One minute of show usually needs 100 minutes of preparation (travelling time not counted). And it is an immensely creative task. I am time and time again awestruck that the emotional message of a certain footage or sequence of pictures can be almost completely overturned by using a different kind of music with it. Again, the inspiring part is to use this medium with all its supporting tools to interact with and entertain a specific audience—in this case, usually friends and relatives, or just about anybody who cares to see my material. This Christmas, more than twenty people came to my place to see my most recent show; Christmas showtime is now a five year old tradition. They seem to like it.

The third context is the one which, unfortunately, is the most rare in my consultant life: On-stage performance. Due to my unsteady consultant lifestyle, I lost contact with my amateur theatre group. The more eager I am to be on stage during (Big Consulting Company), activities. For the recent (Big Consulting Company) outing, I wrote a sketch as a part of a complete show and coached its cast, including myself. It certainly was the most fun thing I have done for (Big Consulting Company) during the last year. I feel especially satisfied at the fact the the whole cast (all on stage for the first time in their lifes, recruited from all ranks and functions within (Big Consulting Company) loved the experience and the audience enjoyed our play.

This is why I love to entertain an audience. This immense satisfaction at adding instant value to people's lifes. The euphoria a successful performance creates in both the entertained and the entertaining. And I am positive it has very often inspired new approaches to issues at work in me which helped me solve my problems.

Comments

This essay is interesting because it is different. Not many candidates would have presented this topic and they would have lost a good opportunity to set themselves apart. This writer recognized the validity of his hobby. In tackling it, he shows himself to be unusual and, true to his word, entertaining. He convinces the committee members that his picture shows do take a good deal of time and creative energy to produce. Therefore, they are probably a good deal more interesting than the usual postvacation, living room slide show.

ESSAY 23: Tuck, multiple activities
What interests do you have outside your job and school?

Perhaps due to my father's strong influence on my development, my greatest interest outside work is educating myself. After focusing narrowly on business in school, my father taught himself European history and art over several years. Under his tutelage, I, too, gained a genuine appreciation for those topics. I read complex history texts at a young age and traveled to Europe with my family several times. I still enjoy reading art history, mythology, and period histories so that I have a greater understanding each time I travel abroad. Travel is exhilarating because it is my opportunity to be adventuresome and discover new places and people, in addition to giving me a healthier, more educated perspective on the world.

Although some friends are quick to label me a "dork," I also enjoy reading about certain areas of science. My father and I used to exercise our minds by reading about quantum physics and astronomy. We enjoyed testing our layman's understanding of complex theoretical concepts while gardening or shooting baskets. Recently, I have branched out and read about the emerging sciences surrounding complexity and chaos. I am not a rocket scientist as a result, but I see the wisdom of my father's advice to retain a healthy intellectual curiosity and expand my thinking beyond the realm of work. Doing so has sharpened my mind and improved my perspective.

Beyond spending precious little time with friends dining out, shopping, or going to movies, I also enjoy many forms of exercise, including ocean kayaking, skiing, and mountain climbing. To date, I have climbed nearly two dozen significant peaks in North America. In addition, I very much enjoy Baroque classical music and opera. Unfortunately, my music career ended unceremoniously with the recorder in fourth grade, and my greatest accomplishment in music remains having sung [karaoke].

Although these activities are, by most measures, unremarkable, continuing to learn about a variety of topics and remaining broad are important to me. Consulting is an engrossing job that demands much of my time. Unfortunately, my travel schedule for work has prevented any consistent involvement in community or volunteer activities outside the context of [consulting firm]. Over the past three years, I have been out of town four to five days a week, approximately forty-five weeks per year. Although I enjoyed tutoring others while in college, such activities are impossible with my current schedule. However, I recognize the trade-offs I have made. I am proud that I have worked very hard at [consulting firm], and it has helped me achieve many of my aggressive career goals.

Comments

This is a good example of a typical candidate who has many interests and tries to do justice to all of them. Although this approach is not as effective in making the writer memorable, it does stress his many positive attributes and leaves the reader with a good overall impression. He could have done without the self-depreciation, though. One wonders, for example, why he feels a need to define his activities as unremarkable after listing the fairly impressive range of nonprofessional interests and activities. No one would have thought this about him if the writer had not introduced it himself. He could also have refrained from calling himself a dork. The essayist probably meant to be humorous. This could have worked if the overall tone of the essay supported it. Instead, the word stands out awkwardly, making the reader question the writer's confidence.

CHAPTER 11

Role Models

> • Your role models say a lot about your values.
>
> • It is best to choose someone with whom you have a direct relationship.
>
> • Cite specific experiences with this individual that have impacted your personal or professional development.

Business schools learn a lot about your professional development through your description of your mentors. They can determine not only what you have learned but the types of people from whom you have learned. However, like the accomplishments question, this question shows a lot about your values and standards. It is a little like getting to know a person by the people with whom he or she chooses to spend time. If you are skeptical, consider the different impression you would have of the candidate who admires a dynamic, colorful, public leader compared with someone who looks up to an accomplished but soft-spoken academic.

Who you choose is more important than how you portray that person. In other words, do not choose a person because you think it will impress the committee. Name dropping is not only obvious, it is ineffective. If your mentor is a public figure, be sure to demonstrate that you have a real, direct relationship with and that you learned tangible lessons from the person. Keep your essay short and simple. Never elevate your mentor at the expense of yourself. Show admiration, not awe. In other words, choose a mentor, not a hero. A mentor is someone whom you realistically aspire to emulate, whereas a hero's qualities are beyond our reach.

If the question calls for more than one mentor, try comparing two different people or people from two unrelated areas of your life. Show how you incorporated the best pieces of wisdom from both. As always, use concrete examples both when describing these people and when demonstrating the effect they have had on you. Do more than list their qualities—tell a story that shows how they have put these qualities to use.

You can follow these steps to structure this essay:

1. Introduce the person and the context in which you know him or her.

2. Describe a few of the mentor's key qualities that you most admire.

3. Relate one or two particular scenarios that demonstrate these qualities.

4. Describe what you have learned from the person. What do you now do differently as a result of having known your mentor? How have you or your actions changed?

Be concrete. Cite specific examples of things that you have learned. Describe the situations in which you learned these things. Show how you have used this knowledge to your professional advantage.

The two essays presented last are a little different. They answer the question, "If you could walk in someone else's shoes for a day . . . ." This is a cross between an ideal career question and a role model question. Whereas the other role model questions ask for mentors, this question asks for heroes. You do not need to make your response as realistic—feel free to loosen up and have fun. However, always consider what committee members will infer from your choice. Answer this question more concisely than you would the role model one. Simply state who you would choose and answer why. Did you choose this person because he or she is similar or dissimilar to you? Did you choose your mentor for what you can learn from that person or to effect a change? Would you ever seriously consider this person's life as a career, or are you just having fun?

ESSAY 24: Michigan, politics, philanthropy
Describe the individuals that you look up to as role models in your professional work.

There are two individuals who have deeply shaped my professional thinking. They are individuals who epitomize the ability to create opportunity and quality in the world around them. These are individuals who have a creative energy others seems to lack, a willingness to explore the unexplored, and an uncanny ability to create enthusiasm and opportunity.

The first, was a mentor of mine in college named [name]. [Name] was respected, not only for his intellect but for his creativity, high standards and persistent ability to challenge students to think beyond their traditional assumptions. Although [name] is a nationally recognized author, he still made time to teach a class specifically reserved for first year students, he sponsored campus-wide debates on local public issues, challenged other professors to take academic advising more seriously and wrote extensively about what it takes to be an excellent teacher in addition to being a scholar. People like [name] are rare. They have a unique ability to challenge the familiar without straying so far as to alienate others. There is a rigor to this kind of approach to life that I have tried to adopt.

A second person who has captured my attention for his unique presence and ability to "create reality" is my present boss, Governor [name]. Three years ago, I took a position as a junior policy analyst because it was a great opportunity to work for a governor who shared my political views. I now realize that this has been a unique opportunity to work, not only for a governor, but for this particular governor.

Governor [name] thinks intuitively outside the box. His advice to me is often "If it ain't broke, break it." A business man and entrepreneur at heart, the Governor is tireless at finding new, more effective ways to hold public institutions accountable for their product, to push for efficiencies and new approaches to solving real problems, rather than just "rearranging the shells." Governor [name]'s straight-forward focus on getting beyond talking about the problem to actually solving it and his willingness to push unpopular issues or approaches to get there are a sign of real courage and a reason for his effectiveness. Governor [name] creates room for change in a system built to resist it.

The people who have most influenced me, however, likely do not know the impact they have had on my thinking. They are the people I work with in my various volunteer and philanthropic activities. My contact with some of these people pushes me to figure out how I can apply my creative, problem solving energy to real needs in my community.

In college, I ran a mentoring program that paired college students with area middle school children who had been identified as being at risk of dropping out of school. The program combined organized educational opportunities with structured tutoring and mentoring and eventually incorporated more than 200 children and about as many mentors. I work now as a tutor for a second grade student living in public housing near my office. I teach as an instructor in a downhill skiing program for disabled children and I have worked as an instructor for a rock climbing program for the blind.

While I feel that I have a lot to teach, more often I am the one who draws most from these experiences. Working with young kids in need and with individuals whose challenges in life are much greater than my own give me a grounding, a sense of humility and sense of patience with my own world that are hard to find anywhere else. I believe these experiences help to keep my professional focus from straying too far from those who actually receive the services of my work. These experiences drive me to ask what can be done to creatively build bridges that might give many of the people I encounter access to opportunities that may otherwise be deprived of them by an inhumane private market. They ground me in a commitment to public service and a sense of urgency to find new approaches to stubborn old problems. I see that our world is too willing to stereotype, too willing to cast people and communities into boxes designed for a "one-size-fits-all" mentality and that those who make a difference in the community or in a business, are those who can think—and act, outside the box.

Comments

This applicant has achieved a nice balance by choosing one mentor from his academic life, one from his professional life, and one from his extracurricular life. His first two examples emphasize that he admires creative and dynamic individuals who are willing to swim against the stream. His third example tells us more about himself than about his students. It risks falling into the cliché, "I've learned more from my students than they've learned from me." The last sentence saves it from triteness by crediting his positive volunteer experience to "thinking outside the box," which he learned from his first two mentors. This ties all three examples together while, at the same time, showing that the essayist has acted on the lessons he learned.

ESSAY 25: Tuck, management consulting

Describe the characteristics of an exceptional manager by examining someone whom you have observed or with whom you have worked. Illustrate how his or her management style has influenced you.

In management consulting, strong analytical skills are valued as much as, if not more than, effective managerial and leadership skills. Unfortunately, for some consultants, these characteristics, at times, are mutually exclusive. I was fortunate, however, to work with [name] on my first major project at [consulting firm]. As my project manager, he demonstrated a superior combination of leadership, managerial, and communication skills. As a result of our interaction, I learned several important lessons and tools that I used on subsequent projects to improve my effectiveness as a team leader.

To begin, [name] is a true leader who exhibits courage and dedication. A powerful trait rarely found in the realm of business, courage is unique in its ability to unify and motivate people. Moreover, his courage is balanced appropriately with professionalism, strong values, and humility. He is sensitive to others' feelings and recognizes that different people require different types of direction and treatment. Although he often works with diverse and difficult groups, he always seems able to reach consensus and create a shared vision and purpose. Furthermore, he excels at establishing priorities and proactively setting direction.

As an effective manager, [name] also is able to translate his broad direction into discrete, tangible tasks. Since consultants often use difficult or creative analytical approaches, clearly articulating tasks and defining outputs is very important. In addition, he exercises the appropriate level of supervision. Rather than micro-managing his team members, [name] establishes clear accountabilities and expectations and pushes work down to the correct level. As a result, he creates a strong sense of ownership and leverages the skills of his team members. Furthermore, he excels at creating a supportive environment and, when necessary, coaching team members to help them develop new skills.

Finally, [name] is a masterful communicator. He is the only project manager I have had who gave me consistent and constructive feedback, importantly, both positive and negative. Such feedback not only provides clear developmental objectives, but also signals to others that he values their contributions. This type of balanced and open communication quickly forms the foundation of mutual trust and respect. Furthermore, [name] excels in the art of negotiation and debate. He states his points with remarkable precision and is expert at remaining objective and recognizing all sides of an argument. And, regardless of the volatility of a situation or the strength of his feelings, he always listens to all positions patiently and effectively controls his demonstration of emotion, thereby gaining the respect of others and lending additional credibility to his positions.

Given my limited experience managing teams, my exposure to [name] was central to my early success at [consulting firm]. For example, although I had considered myself a leader in athletics, I had not learned to translate those skills into the business arena. [Name] taught me several effective methods to lead teams. Admittedly, as a highly motivated young analyst with very high work standards, I also lacked many of the skills required for effective team leadership. However, I quickly learned the importance of flexibility and became more comfortable providing feedback and directing the work of others. Furthermore, through his example, [name] taught me the importance of objectivity and the utility of several effective communication techniques. For example, I learned to use my sense of humor as an effective tool to persuade, disarm, or motivate others.

Early in my career at [consulting firm], I had several rare opportunities to lead client teams. In part due to the lessons I learned from [name], these projects were a great success. As a result, I went on to manage a half dozen diverse and difficult client teams that ranged in membership. With each project, I further refined the lessons I learned from [name] and developed new techniques for leading and managing teams. Due to my rapid development, I was promoted to [position], a managerial, post-M.B.A. position at [consulting firm], signifying that I can progress to the partner level. Although I realize my tool kit is far from complete, these skills will be invaluable both in business school and beyond.

Comments

This is another essay that stands out because of its solid writing and superior organization. It starts with a bold assertion to catch the reader's attention and then uses the assertion to introduce the mentor's most outstanding quality. Each of the next three paragraphs clearly asserts and describes an additional supporting quality. The essay concludes with examples of how the mentor's influence has tangibly affected the writer's actions and work performance, resulting in rapid promotion.

ESSAYS 26 and 27: Chicago, essay comparison

If you could walk in someone else's shoes for a day, whose would you choose and why?

Conventional wisdom suggests that walking in the shoes of someone like Bill Gates or Steve Jobs or Louis Gerstner, Jr. would be the ideal way to spend a day. What better way to pass the day than as the C.E.O. of one of the world's largest corporations, with thousands of people looking to you for visionary leadership, right? Although this type of experience does have some appeal to me, if I only had one day to spend, I would rather be Troy Aikman, quarterback of the Dallas Cowboys.

As a professional football player, Troy lives in a world somewhat removed from the boardrooms of a Fortune 500 C.E.O. But what is appealing to me about Troy is the way he combines a successful career in professional football with successful business interests outside of football, and yet still retains his genuine, humble personality. Recognized almost unanimously as the premier on-field leader in his sport, Troy has set the example of what it takes to be a winner in his profession and has led his team to two championships. In addition, Troy has his own company, Aikman Enterprises, through which he manages his many business interests, including several successful real estate ventures in the Dallas area. As an example of his exemplary character, Troy was one of the first contributors to the disaster relief fund in Oklahoma City after the April 19th bombing, donating $10,000 to the effort.

I choose to be Troy Aikman for a day not for his $50 million salary package, not for his looks, and not for his popularity. I choose him for what he represents: a genuine, down-to-earth person whose hard work and unceasing committment to personal and team success has not tarnished his concern for others. There are too many examples in today's world of men and women who became successful in business or other careers, only to be spoiled by their successes. I have no doubt that I, too, will be successful at whatever I choose to do. I hope that I can be just as humble and just as giving as Troy Aikman.

If you could walk in someone else's shoes for a day, whose would you choose and why?

Although it is tempting to select Michael Jordan of the Chicago Bulls, to experience the thrill he enjoys as the most talented member of his field, the insight gained by spending a day as Bill Gates would be the most interesting, educational, and useful to my future. Mr. Gates, co-founder and C.E.O. of Microsoft, is one of the most visionary and active individuals of our time.

The opportunity to explore his vision for the future is fascinating. Many of his thoughts, detailed in his recently published *The Road Ahead*, reveal a brilliant mind years ahead of the most current technology. As an avid computer enthusiast myself, I would enjoy realizing his personal thoughts as to what he perceives as possible and feasible in the future. To which pursuits is he devoting the greatest research and development efforts? What is his strategy concerning the Internet? What evolution will possibly follow the Internet? The opportunity for answers to these and other questions via a look into the future through Bill Gates' sight would allow me to most effectively plan for and utilize future technological innovations.

In addition to satisfying my curiosity of what the future might possibly hold, the insight gained through his personal experience founding and growing his corporation would be personally very valuable. Whereas the world now views Mr. Gates as a billionaire corporate tycoon, I would appreciate insight into the concerns and difficulties he encountered along the way. The individual issues he encountered, including choosing partners and financial contributors, whom he trusted and whom disappointed him, and other personal issues would prepare me for similar struggles I may find along my entrepreneurial journey. A day in Bill Gates' shoes would satisfy my intellectual curiosity as well as offer pragmatic insight directly applicable to my future aspirations.

Comments

These two essays were chosen partially to prove that what you write about does not matter. Instead, how you write about it and what you let it say about you matters. These two applicants took completely opposing topics and wrote in direct contrast to one another. Yet both essays work fine.

CHAPTER 12

Failure

- Answer this question honestly and humbly.
- Do not turn it into a success story without first admitting your failure.
- The most important part of your response is demonstrating what you learned and how you have evolved.

Any applicant who tries to claim or assert perfection on the application would, at best, be treated as a joke. No one is perfect, and no admissions committee expects perfection. Yet, more than any other question, this one strikes fear into the hearts of applicants. However, answering this question does not need to be difficult. You must get past the biggest hurdle—your own reticence.

Failure often results from good intentions and admirable qualities such as initiative, leadership, and risk taking. Take advantage of the fact that failure will sometimes result from our best qualities. Any leader who has tried to forge a new path has made a mistake somewhere along the way. If you are honest and forthright about the mistake you made, people will remember the intention over the result. Besides, the committee is not interested in judging you on your mistake, they simply want to know how you dealt with it. The only real way to flunk this question is to dodge it. If you choose a trite or irrelevant topic, the committee will either question your honesty and your maturity or doubt your ability to lead, take risks, and think outside the box.

If you are having trouble choosing a situation, consider the following guidelines:

1. Choose something that has happened recently. Delving too far into your past is an obvious cop-out.

2. Do not limit yourself to professional failures, but do not shy away from them either. Admissions committees are aware of the risk inherent in choosing job failures and will give you points for being forthright.

3. Do not choose anything overly dramatic or that would call your morals into question. The reader should be able to relate to your failure, not be shocked by it.

If you cannot clearly state what you learned from the incident or the actions that you took to amend it, then pick something else. When you are writing, take a simple, straightforward, objective tone. Do not try to excuse your actions. Let your story speak for itself. Keep your essay as concise as possible.

ESSAY 28: Harvard, consulting, recruiting failure
To recognize that effective managers are able to learn from failure, describe a failure that you have experienced. What did you learn from the experience?

At The Boston Consulting Group (BCG), Mark, the partner in charge of associate recruiting, asked me to organize a minority recruiting presentation at Harvard and Yale. He was concerned about our lack of African-American associates and wanted to increase awareness of BCG among the minority community. Both Harvard and Yale have Afro-American organizations, and I enlisted their help in organizing the event.

I made several key mistakes with the Yale presentation. I was busy with my casework and was not as diligent in getting started as I should have been. It took me several weeks to get in touch with the person, Marisa, who was in charge of business outreach at the Afro-Am center. When I finally did get in touch with her, we did not have many choices for a date on which to hold the event, because of finals, Thanksgiving vacation and Mark's and my schedules. I was forced to settle for 4:00 on a weekday, not a particularly auspicious time for an event like this. I knew that many people would be working in the dining halls, at practice, or just plain tired after a day of classes.

I made my second mistake when publicizing the event. Instead of preparing a blitz of publicity, with flyers in people's mailboxes and posters all over campus, I settled for what Marisa had time to organize. She put up some posters and information on campus, but didn't have the time to do any more.

When Mark, another associate and I drove down to New Haven for our presentation, we found an embarrassingly small turnout. There were only four people and one of them was a junior who wanted to know if we had any summer jobs. We all felt discouraged with the results of our efforts. I realized that I should have called up friends of mine still at Yale and paid them to publicize the event. I also could have taken out an advertisement in the *Yale Daily News*.

After the disastrous turnout at Yale, I did the only thing I could do: make certain that the same thing didn't happen at Harvard. First of all,

Harvard's schedule gave me a few extra weeks with which to work, and I was able to arrange the presentation for 7:30 on a weekday, which was the perfect time. More importantly, I made a concerted effort to publicize the event, even sending out direct mailings to minority students.

This time, things went as I had hoped. Sixteen or seventeen people showed up, all of whom were extremely interested in consulting, and many of whom ended up applying to BCG.

This was my first rude awakening to the experience of organizing something that involved relying on other people. It taught me that the Boy Scouts have the right idea: "Always be prepared!" Over and over, at work and at YAAMNY, I see the importance of planning ahead and taking every measure possible to ensure something's success.

Comments

This essayist picked a perfect situation for the essay. She chose a relevant topic from her professional life but not one that seriously questions her values. Everyone can relate to letting responsibilities slide, and the reader sympathizes with her discouragement and embarrassment when the first event fails. The writer also does a good job of recognizing what mistakes she made—lack of preparation as well as lack of publicity. The real strength of this essay, though, is the essayist's focus on how she used the lessons she learned to organize the second event. The fact that she had tangible results reflects very well on her ability to persevere and succeed.

Essay 29: Harvard, squash failure

To recognize that effective managers are able to learn from failure, describe a failure that you have experienced. What did you learn from the experience?

Squash is a strange game, one in which success is at least as dependent upon mental ability as it is on physical attributes. Like other sports, physical gifts can expedite success in squash, but in the end it is discipline and continual hard work that is necessary in order to achieve a player's true potential. Endless hours of hitting a small black ball in an empty room, all the while having no discernible objective, is the only way to improvement for the dedicated squash player.

The Squash League is a favorite after-work activity of mine; the competition is intense and of high-quality, but the matches also present a pleasant opportunity to unwind and meet other people from around the city. Traditionally, the club I play for is one of the better sides in the city, and we all treat winning and losing in a fairly serious manner. So it came as a shock and a disappointment when I lost a crucial squash match for my club. What made it particularly frustrating was that the match was an important play-off against a player I had beaten numerous times. I recall thinking about this several times during the loss, and wondering what was different about this time. No matter what shot I hit, or how I altered my serves, my opponent seemed to be everywhere at once; I was on and off the court in a matter of minutes, not knowing what had hit me.

There is something else about squash that makes it different from the other sports and activities in which I usually participate: it is an individual sport, and the credit for success or the onus of failure is usually directly attributable to one person. I lost that match, and there was no one else to shoulder any part of the blame. Internally, I replayed what had happened and wondered why I had failed to defeat someone whom I had beaten every other time we had met. I had walked onto the court in an ridiculously confident manner; losing was not a viable option to me. Thinking about that made me realize that my overconfidence was not a recent phenomenon; I had been complacent and presumptuous on the topic of my squash game all along. Instead of devoting the effort necessary to improve my abilities, I had grown unduly satisfied, and been content with my level of development. While I had been resting on my laurels, my opponent had been practicing to ensure that my occupation of the top position would be short-lived.

The consequences of my disregard for discipline and hard work, two central tenets of self-improvement, were both an embarrassing loss for myself and a letdown for my teammates, and what I learned can be easily applied to many personal or professional situations. Appreciation of the importance of continuous self-improvement and not taking anything for granted are the lessons this failure left me, and I believe that these valuable legacies were worth my failure.

Comments

This writer chooses the common and safe fallback of an athletic failure—a typical response to this question. He takes accountability for his failure and understands the reasons why he lost the game, which are good. His essay could have been better, though. Instead of simply saying that he has learned from the experience, he should have included an example of, perhaps, the next game he won. Then, the essayist should have explained why it resulted from the actions he took after learning his lessons. As it is, this essay is pretty neutral—it probably did not help him much, but neither did it hurt him.

ESSAY 30: Harvard, sorority fund-raising failure

To recognize that effective managers are able to learn from failure, describe a failure that you have experienced. What did you learn from the experience?

As Philanthropy Chair for my college sorority, I coordinated community service activities and major fundraising events. My first major fund-raiser flopped, and the experience highlighted the importance of collective commitment.

I wanted our new sorority to develop a positive, philanthropic reputation. So, I pressed the philanthropy committee to develop a fund-raiser for early spring semester, in addition to a late spring event. The committee, lacking other ideas, grudgingly decided to make and sell green, mint-chocolate-flavored shamrock lollipops for St. Patrick's Day.

The lack of commitment was evident from the beginning. No one was willing to pick up supplies. Getting volunteers—from over 100 sorority members—to make the pops was virtually impossible, leaving a few reluctant committee members to melt, mold, and wrap hundreds of chocolates. Members were disinclined to sell the candy; some simply bought their entire allocation. To increase sales, we set up a table outside the student union, but unseasonably high temperatures melted the remaining pops into shapeless blobs, which we sold at a discount.

The fund-raiser clearly did not bolster our philanthropic reputation, nor did it increase sorority members' passion for service. I realized that my arbitrary process goal (number of events per semester) limited substantive results. I saw the importance of garnering commitment early, and of matching events with the level of dedication. We raised about $400, so from a financial perspective, the fund-raiser was not a complete failure. Nevertheless, I felt responsible for the dismal results: a lesson in the burden of leadership.

We chose subsequent philanthropic activities more carefully. With selected visible, single-day events, members participated in the fun, interactive activity for a limited, expected time. Lessons from the St. Patty's Pops experience enabled us to raise thousands of dollars through other events.

Comments

As stated before, failure often results from good intentions, leadership, and initiative. This writer has chosen a failure that demonstrates all three. The fact that she made her mistakes is not as important as the fact that she tried. The only real risk this writer took was in choosing an event that took place in the context of a college sorority, which could have easily appeared trite. However, she pulls it off by making the essay real and by writing sincerely.

CHAPTER 13

Ethical Dilemmas

- Responses to this question should convey your values and decision-making skills.

- Focus on how you dealt with the given situation more than on the dilemma itself.

- Avoid experiences that depict you as subordinate or noncontributory as a team member.

Many people see this question as being similar to the failure question. In reality, it is closer to the leadership question. Use this to your advantage, especially if you are having trouble thinking of a topic. We are often called to lead when a difficult decision must be made. Most ethical dilemmas are just difficult decisions disguised with an intimidating name. The reason that this question is not as similar to the failure question is that here you need only to have deliberated over a sticky situation, not to have actually failed in response to one. The ethical dilemma question allows you to emphasize your strong values and morals; the failure question does just the opposite.

The main purpose of this essay is not to find out the kind of dilemmas you have dealt with but to see how you have responded to them. Approach the subject candidly. Show that your principles were tested but that passed. A strong person stands up for what he or she believes—this quality is a sure sign of a leader.

Watch out for a couple of pitfalls, though. Try not to choose a situation where your loyalty to a boss or manager could be called into question. Directly disobeying a boss's orders can demonstrate leadership—but can also highlight a few not so positive traits as well, such as poor teamwork. Also, show that you upheld your principles, but try not to cross the line into rigidity or stubbornness. A good manager is someone who can work well with a lot of people—even people who have different opinions and viewpoints.

ESSAY 31: Harvard, investment banking
Describe an ethical dilemma you experienced firsthand. How did you manage and resolve the situation?

Last April, my company was repeatedly contacted by the management team of a factory in [city], who presented their company as a potential [deal] prospect. However, our prior investigations had classified the company as an also-ran, without great potential for improvement. We reasoned that a visit would be a waste of time and served no viable business purpose, but wondered: why not utilize this opportunity to wring industry information out of the factory? Afterwards, we could simply state our lack of interest with no loss on [company]'s part except travel expenses. Looking back, I recognized the dishonesty inherent in my team's motives, but rationalized that the cover of being interested in the factory was a professional necessity. In any case, no one would be hurt, or so we surmised.

Most of the visit went smoothly; under the guise of interested investors, we toured the factory and interviewed management, laying the groundwork for negotiations that I knew would never occur. The factory manager was extremely responsive in providing answers and was a gracious host, toasting us with eloquent speeches at dinner. Afterwards, as we prepared to return to our hotel to arrange the next day's travel, he surprised us by announcing a special post-dinner presentation. Following a short car ride down a deserted dirt road, we were brought to a ominous, isolated building and led inside. As we walked through the door, I recall nervously questioning what we were doing there and wondering if the factory had somehow learned of our true disinterested nature.

The first thing I noticed inside the building were the five hundred men, women and children in the room standing and applauding us; we were led to the seats nearest to the stage. Immediately, a group of young girls, perhaps ten years old, shuffled onto the stage and began to chime "song 1" and "song 2" in broken, but perfectly understandable English. The program on the table in front of me detailed a list of art demonstrations, comedy routines, and musical/dance exhibitions which were to be performed by troupes of workers and their families. The two-hour show displayed a great deal of time and effort and was truly one of the most special, and painful, memories from my time in [country].

I remember my ensuing letter of rejection to the factory with a sense of regret. I wish I could say I managed this dilemma well, but I realize that I failed to account for the fact that [country] factories are more social, educational and vocational unit than workplace. By not giving thought to the consequences of our actions, my team had caused wasted effort and dashed hopes. Through this, I have learned a valuable lesson on integrating business and ethics, and have vowed to utilize this insight into all of the decisions I make.

Comments

This is an amazingly heartfelt and powerful portrayal. It took courage to deal with such a sensitive issue in this context. It is also an example of someone who chose a situation where they made the wrong choice. Because the writer did this, the same essay could be used to answer a failure question. Despite the fact that he made the wrong choice, the writer proves himself to be a person of real feeling. The reader is left with no doubt that the regret the essayist feels is real and that he will not make a similar mistake again.

ESSAY 32: Harvard, investment banking
Describe an ethical dilemma you experienced firsthand. How did you manage and resolve the situation?

I worked on an equity offering for a Houston-based client with whom [investment bank] had built a very strong working relationship. The deal started off well, with the client proving very easy to work with. As I spent more time down in Houston, however, I began to feel less comfortable with the client personnel. All senior management, in fact all management that I encountered in their offices, were Caucasian men. I began to realize that the only minorities visible worked in maintenance or as security guards or kitchen staff. Outside of the secretaries, the only woman I ever saw in my two months working there was the analyst who helped me build the financial models. I also noticed with curiosity that the African American woman on our team never came to Houston to meet with the client.

This odd situation came to a head late in the deal during a lunch I attended in the executive dining room. Sequestered behind closed doors, the informal chatter between company officials became lively and, to my surprise and discomfort, peppered with derogatory remarks and jokes about women, about minorities, about foreigners. These men didn't seem to care that I was myself from a minority background, perhaps they expected me to laugh along with them. I did not.

I spent that evening in my hotel room wondering how I could, and if I should, continue working for clients with such prejudice, whose behavior made me very uncomfortable. Ultimately I decided that I have an individual right to decline even those projects which [investment bank] as an institution accepts, but that I had a professional responsibility to my teammates and to the firm to complete the final stages of a project I had started two months earlier. I further resolved to recommend to the relationship manager that [investment bank] review its position as a business partner to this client.

The next day I discussed my concerns with the client manager, reminding him that [former chairman] had unequivocally stated the firm's motto as "[motto]". Helping promote and strengthen businesses and leaders who have an inherent disrespect for women and minorities was certainly not first class business, and participating in such activity was against everything that [name] stood for. Understanding the delicate nature of his position, I offered my opinion that arguments of profitability, relationship, and "if we don't do this someone else will," were unsound in light of the ethical issues and very real reputational risks for the firm.

True to my convictions, I did all of my work from New York during the last few weeks of this project and skipped the closing dinner in Houston later that month. When the senior client manager asked me to join his team permanently at the end of this assignment, I declined gracefully. Six months later the client re-hired us for another assignment, and although both the client and [investment bank] requested that I work on the project for relationship reasons, this too I refused.

Appropriately enough, this client is currently under compliance review at [investment bank], signaling a possible end to the relationship.

Comments

This candidate demonstrates both that he has strong ethical standards and that he knows where to draw the line in allowing them to rule his judgments. He was right to stand up for his convictions but also right to have deliberated and kept his cool as long as he did. This essay shows him to be upstanding as well as levelheaded. Had he flown off the handle at any point or sabotaged a client relationship without due consideration and counsel, he would have come off as bullheaded and rash.

ESSAY 33: Harvard, homeless volunteer

Describe an ethical dilemma you experienced firsthand. How did you manage and resolve the situation?

To be quite honest, I have fortunately not been faced with a grave ethical dilemma in either my professional or personal life. However, I believe we all face a multitude of subtle ethical dilemmas every day that affect us in varying degrees. The dilemma that I wrestle with most often is not unique, my response is not heroic, and the situation may never actually be resolved. However, tired of being passive, I have taken action in my own personal way to resolve my ethical dilemma.

If you live in an urban setting, you pass homeless people on the street or in the subway every day. How many of us walk by them and wage an internal battle whether to reach into our pocket and give them some change? Some people don't. They have a set policy that they don't give money to people on the street, or they have a set policy that they always do. Others will give, but only if they can walk across the street with that person and buy them a cup of coffee or some food. I'm not one of those people with a set policy. I can honestly say that I never know until the person is directly in front of me whether I will give. Each time, I have a very unsettling, 3-4 second period of indecision in which I try with obvious lack of success to weigh each facet of my dilemma. Will this person use my money toward food or toward one more drink? Am I contributing to his/her problems or am I helping someone who is down on his/her luck? Why is this person homeless? Is he/she able to work if given the chance? Sometimes I give, more often I don't. I simply have never been able to decide whether my contribution will be beneficial. When I graduated from college and moved into the city, my dilemma obviously became more acute, as did my indecision.

How did I resolve the dilemma? I decided not to decide. There was no set policy that could answer my key concern. However, I took a course of action I could confirm was indisputably beneficial, and although it would not resolve the homeless problem, it would go a long way towards resolving my personal ethical dilemma. Putnam has a program established with the Boston Night Center, a homeless shelter near North Station. I started as a volunteer, and now am Team Captain. Every two weeks, the Team Captain recruits six members of our department to go to the supermarket to buy food, use the shelter's kitchen to prepare the meal, serve the food, and then clean up. The whole process begins at 6 P.M. and is usually over by 11 P.M. The most difficult part of the job is motivating 6 people who work sixty to seventy hours a week to spend an extra six hours giving time to others. For me, it is the perfect way to resolve my dilemma. There is no debate as to the merit of your actions when you are at the shelter. It is obvious that the results are positive. To be honest, the motivation is not totally unselfish in that you can witness the immediate gratification that the shelter residents receive, and you sense their appreciation.

I don't pretend to believe that I do nearly enough to help the cause of the homeless, or even that I am doing all that I can. I still give to some homeless people on the street and not to others. There is still doubt in my mind when I walk by someone and don't help. However, I have taken an ethical dilemma that was personal to me, and am working toward resolving it. That is a step.

Comments

This topic choice would have been pegged as an easy way out had the writer's subsequent course of action not proven her sincerity. However, the fact that she became Team Captain of a homeless shelter volunteer group removes any doubt about the strength of her convictions. She writes in a wonderfully simple and candid manner. The portrayal of her decision paints a picture of a sensitive person who takes action and initiative in response to a universally uncomfortable and difficult situation.

CHAPTER 14

Getting Personal

(Personal Development, Personal Goals, Background and Influence)

- Personal questions beg you to let down your guard and reveal yourself.

- Select the most important traits that you wish to reveal—don't try to include everything.

All essay questions, as we have already mentioned, are a way for the admissions committee to learn more about you personally. The getting personal questions just ask more directly than others. They give you a direct opportunity to speak for yourself. They can be tricky, though, because they are often extremely open-ended.

Be selective. You cannot include every detail about yourself, so you have to pick wisely. Some applicants want to tell everything, fearful that they will leave out a crucial detail on which their acceptance, and future, could hinge. Do not give in to this temptation. Instead, focus on one or two significant qualities or characteristics that give the admissions committee genuine insight into you.

Many of the questions in this category are worded creatively or ask you to use your imagination. This is intended to get you to loosen up and be yourself. If the question takes you off guard, let it—it means the committee is looking for an unguarded answer. This makes many applicants uncomfortable. They try to present themselves objectively but end up distancing themselves from the subject matter with overly long words and a dry, academic tone. This is a grave mistake since the whole point of this essay is to reveal something about yourself. Therefore, put your heart into this essay.

This category does not have one standard question—every school asks it in a different way. Although each school's question will differ from the next, most of the personal questions still fit into one of three categories: personal development, personal goals, or personal background and influence. If you are having trouble with a specific question, try to approach it from the vantage point of one of these categories. See if the tips and advice given below help.

Personal Development

- Highlight one or two significant events and how you have changed as a result of them.
- Take credit for your changes and development.

This question tries to find out about you by asking how you have grown and developed over the past few years. Making you compare yourself at two different stages of your life is a clever way to get you to open up about who you really are. Although you do want to show that you have matured, remember that the child is father of the man. Do not overplay what a terrible person you once were just to make the point of what a great person you are now. No one changes that much in five years. Do, however, highlight one or two turning points or significant events, and show how they have affected you. They need not be dramatic, just personally meaningful. Also remember to show that you took a proactive as well as a reactive role in your own development. How did your growth result from the decisions you made and the actions you took? Significant events and people can serve as inspiration, but real change always results from the work, effort, and initiative you have put into yourself. Take credit for your hard work!

ESSAY 34: Sloan, humorous, general
If we had met you five years ago and then met you again today, how would we say that you have changed? Include specific examples that characterize your development.

Five years ago I was twenty years old, just finishing up my first semester of my sophomore year in school. I had curly blond hair down to my waist and had never worked a full-time job in my life. I had only been out of the country two times. I found the white, preppy uniformity of Georgetown to be familiar and comforting.

Now I live in a rowdy, crazy, colorful, slightly shady neighborhood in Washington, D.C.; I couldn't get out of Georgetown fast enough after graduation. I love to walk down the street and see men in dresses or the Rastas who sit in front of Safeway vending incense and such. I lived and traveled abroad for a full year. I've had a Real Job for over two and a half years. And the further I get from school the more I rediscover a creative spirit that was dormant for four years—I love to paint and draw and write now, which I didn't do at all during college.

But the biggest changes have been in how I relate to my work and the people around me. In the past five years, I learned that the most important achievement in life is to be truly happy. And reaching that goal, for me, required that I try looking at the world with a new view.

I learned how to learn. I was never much of a student—I did the minimum amount of work required to get good grades, and rarely more. That lasted until I was studying at the London School of Economics. The first paper I handed in there came back with a D and comments that indicated the professor felt actual pity and concern for a student of my low caliber. I found out quickly that the study methods I had used throughout my life were not acceptable at the LSE. Rather than just memorizing the notes of the professor's lecture, and my highlighted notes from the textbook, I actually had to use the list of 10–15 books that accompanied each day's lecture, do my own research on the topic, and genuinely understand the concepts in question, backwards and forwards. It was exhilarating. I regretted all the wonderful courses and professors I had wasted in the past. I began my senior year at Georgetown with a new enthusiasm, and ended my fall semester with my first 4.0.

I've learned to enjoy the small moments of joy that every day contains. I've learned that it's okay to pass up one party, because another is sure to come along. Right after my freshman year in school I spent a summer in Boston caring for my sister and her two-year-old son after she had surgery. Basically, every moment I spent in domestic activity was a small hell for me. I was sure that the city held wonders untold, but I was chained inside, cooking, cleaning, grocery shopping, reading "Once Upon A Potty" over and over and over. This year, as I visited my sister for Christmas, I was cast into the Mommy role again when she hurt her knee skiing. This time I relished every minute of it. I played chess with the seven-year-old, and tried to teach the two-month-old to say "Elvis". I delivered cups of tea and bags of ice to my fallen sister, and whipped up a special pot of soup for everyone when we all came down with the same cold. I let my brother-in-law hide in a corner with my nice new laptop. I was actually glad that I barely left the house. I've mellowed out.

I've learned to forgive myself. I'm always my own worst critic, especially when I made mistakes. I could torment myself with a past failure for weeks. But in my current job I've had the chance to fall on my face several times, and to see that the world does not stop turning when I do. One of my bosses has a motto: "Let's turn this negative into a positive"—in his world, there is no failure because there is always a lesson to be learned, at the very least. After a couple of years of being subjected to this unrelenting optimism, I finally yielded and accepted it. I learned that time spent worrying over a mistake is wasted time—instead, I should be figuring out how to correct the mistake and move on.

I've learned to be a positive member of the team. Attitude counts. I will admit that I used to indulge myself in the occasional prima donna fit. I was aware of my value at the company, that there were many things that only I knew how to do, and I played on it to get my way. But this past summer I worked with a vendor, the owner of a mailhouse, who changed my whole way of thinking. Though the work that her company did was timely and basically error-free, dealing with this woman drove me up a wall. She had no concept of customer service—any error that her mailhouse made was somehow our fault. She would not take responsibility for mistakes, she refused to do little things that would have saved us money or made our job easier, and I could never get her off the phone before her life story came out. So even though the mailhouse produced quality work, I will not be using them again next year because working with her was so unpleasant. This taught me an important lesson: it doesn't matter how good your work is—if you're a pain to work with, that's what people remember and react to. Since then I've endeavored to present a consistently pleasant face to my coworkers; whenever I feel a little cranky, I hear the voice of Melissa and just relax.

In five years, I've grown more confident, more secure, and more at ease. I wouldn't say I'm a different person that I was at twenty, but I'm definitely an improved version. Plus—the biggest change of all—I'm a brunette now.

Comments

This writer takes incredible risks—everything from mentioning poor grades and admitting to "prima donna fits" to writing with an unusually funny, informal, and personal tone. However, she pulls it off with spunk, wit, and impressive writing skills. A committee would not soon forget her or her style.

ESSAY 35: Sloan, engineer, religious

If we had met you five years ago and then met you again today, how would we say that you have changed? Include specific examples that characterize your development.

In many respects, my life has changed dramatically in the past five years. They have been years of tremendous growth both personally and professionally. If you had met me five years ago, you would have met a college senior busily planning for life after college. The inevitability of a nine-to-five existence in the "real-world" was fast approaching. However, I did not have a specific career goal apart from simply finding a job as a mechanical engineer. At that time, my only long-term ambitions were to make a six-figure salary and live the "good life". These two particular areas of my life have seen significant changes in the past five years.

First, there is a marked contrast in my career focus between five years ago and today. Five years ago, I was ready to graduate from college with a degree in mechanical engineering but with no clear direction on the specific job function or industry I wanted to pursue. My strategy and decision-making process in finding my first post-college job illustrate this lack of focus. As a job-hunting college senior, I explored employment opportunities with a wide variety of companies. After weighing my choices, I decided to accept a position as an engineer with ABC Company, my current employer and an engineering consulting firm to the power generation industry and the U.S. Navy. While the opportunity to work on interesting and technically challenging projects was enticing, the overriding factor in my decision to accept this position was the opportunity to dabble in a variety of technical disciplines. I shunned all job offers in which I felt that I would be pigeonholed in a particular specialty. In contrast, I now wish to pursue a career specifically as a production engineer for a high technology manufacturing company. In the last couple of years, I have been able to clearly identify my interest in manufacturing through extensive involvement in a specific project to improve the production efficiency of nuclear power plants through the utilization of new digital monitoring system technology.

Another area of my professional life in which I have experienced tremendous growth is my ability to communicate and deal with many different types of people. When I began my career at ABC, my primary role on various teams was to do work in the office to support projects at clients' sites. I had very little direct client contact. Over the past five years, I have been able to hone my communication skills, both written and oral. I have demonstrated these skills to the point where now I am visiting client sites on a regular basis and acting as the primary interface between my firm and some of our clients.

Finally, if you had met me five years ago, you would have found that my life goals were quite different from today. At that time, I can say that I held a rather self-interested life perspective.

My goals were to attain a comfortable life for myself, and to have enough time for my personal leisure. Since then, I have become a Christian, and my new-found faith has been instrumental in turning my value system around and in helping me develop a more balanced lifestyle. One example that illustrates this transformation was my decision to participate in a short-term missionary trip to Guatemala. The purpose of the two-week trip was to help construct a church building in a Pokomchi Indian community. My participation meant that I had to use up my entire two-week annual leave from work. Five years ago, my preference would probably have been to spend that time relaxing on a warm sandy beach.

I most assuredly would not have envisioned myself building a church in a Guatemalan village. Now, while my career and my personal interests are important to me, I have gained a much more balanced perspective on life. It is a perspective which spurs me on toward more active service to my church and to my community.

Comments

Though more typical than the previous essay and not as impeccably crafted, this essay still responds well to this question. The writer demonstrates that he has grown both professionally and personally by using a few specific examples to illustrate each. He mentioned his religious conversion (which can be a difficult subject to handle in this genre) at the right place and used the right tone.

Personal Goals

- Make sure to differentiate your personal goals from your career goals.
- Common topics are family, hobbies, travel, and athletic achievements.
- Include how you plan to achieve your goals.

This question, although worded creatively, really just asks you what goals you have set for your personal life. The only difference is that you will talk about your goals in the past tense, as though they have already happened. The inevitable question here (especially for women) becomes, is it OK to say that I want a family? If that truly is a goal (and it is for most people), then yes, of course you can write about it. Admissions officers have a grasp on reality and they understand that, business person or not, most people end up married and with children. To expect otherwise would be unrealistic and naive.

Not mentioning marriage and family is fine, too. If the subject makes you uncomfortable, leave it out. Because it is expected, it is often left unsaid. You might want to focus instead on one or two unique goals of yours. Do you want to have traveled to a certain place, climbed a specific mountain, or run the Boston Marathon by then? Perhaps you have smaller goals, like learning to play the piano or cook a gourmet meal.

Many people look at their goals from a grander scale by choosing overriding themes like philanthropy and discussing the ways in which they hope the theme will have come into fruition. No matter what you choose, show that you have a realistic goal and not just a pipe dream. Either outline a game plan or prove that you have already taken the first steps toward making the goals come true. Most important of all, do not forget to mention the role that your business career will have had in helping you attain your goals and lead a fulfilling personal life. Goals can be personal and still include your career.

ESSAY 36: Anderson, general

In thirty to forty years, when you reflect back on your life, what criteria will you use when judging if you have been successful? What are the main achievements/events that you hope will have taken place?

As I reflect back on my life, one of the most important indicators of my personal success will be my formation of a family. I hope to have established a successful marriage and to have raised two children emulating the manner in which my parents raised me. If I am able to motivate my children to be active and thoughtful participants in life, and to follow the ethics and values I taught them, then I will have been successful as a mother.

Another indicator of my success will be my establishment of a rewarding and profitable career. Imperative for my personal success is dedicating my life to a career that I enjoy. Also essential is a career through which I will continue to expand my knowledge base, for I have an insatiable thirst for intellectual advancement. As a result of this desire for knowledge, an M.B.A. is an important precursor to a successful career.

As I reflect on my career, I also hope to have worked in another country for a few years. My affinity for foreign languages and cultures is demonstrated by my travel abroad and by a minor in Spanish from a U.C. School. I feel that spending a significant amount of time living and working abroad, preferably in a Spanish-speaking country, would be extremely fulfilling, both personally and professionally.

Yet another of my goals in life is to have blazed new paths for women in business. I would like to have achieved new heights for women in management consulting, serving as a role model for younger women embarking on careers in business. Through my position as a healthcare analyst, I have already begun to dispel some of the prejudices that I find still exist in the workplace. In particular, I have excelled in a quantitative, technologically-driven position in which most of my colleagues are male.

I also hope to have followed my entrepreneurial aspirations by founding my own company. I will undoubtedly be able to judge my professional life as a success if I have started a healthcare consulting practice. Such an endeavor would be challenging, would utilize my diverse talents, and would allow me the flexibility required to spend time with my children. Needless to say, the financial independence that accompanies a successful entrepreneurial venture would be an additional indicator of my overall professional success.

An additional criterion for success in my career is to make a difference in the world. I believe that a profitable career and the betterment of society are not mutually exclusive goals. In my current position with a large consulting firm, I have had numerous opportunities to consult to health-care organizations helping them solve critical financial and operational problems. As I one day look back on my career in the healthcare indus-try, I hope to have played a key role in helping our healthcare delivery system weather its current crisis. Hospitals, more than ever, are compet-ing for patients and must be concerned not only with the quality of care delivered, but also with the cost and efficiency of delivering that care. With the onset of managed care and the downsizing of hospitals na-tionwide, there is an urgent need for managers with both a knowledge of healthcare delivery issues, as well as a solid business management background. I will feel extremely successful if I am able to utilize my knowledge and talents to help healthcare providers become more cost effective and efficient, while maintaining high quality and service levels.

I will also judge my life to have been successful if I am able to use my talents outside of the professional realm to make a significant contribu-tion to philanthropy. I have always felt that a successful career should be accompanied by giving back to the community. I am currently actively involved in Project Read, an adult literacy program. On Wednesday evenings and Saturday mornings, I teach a 31-year-old, unemployed, mother of two to read and write. Every time we meet, I am amazed by my student's determination and delight at every accomplishment, no matter how minor. Her energy and escalating self-confidence at each tutoring session constantly reaffirm my commitment to helping unedu-cated adults, an often overlooked segment of society. I hope to one day look back on my life and to have spent sufficient time extending literacy to as many disadvantaged adults as possible so that they are able to ex-perience the rewards of knowledge that have meant so much to me.

In the end, I feel that the most important prerequisite for a success-ful life is to have made the most of all of the opportunities available to me. Having been fortunate in terms of the education and experiences to which I have had access, I aspire to have a family and career that makes the most of these resources. In 30 to 40 years, I also hope to behold a better world as a result of my talents and efforts, particularly in the area of healthcare.

Comments

This essay is well rounded and shows a good example of a candidate with typical goals. She wants a family with children and admits it upfront but does not dwell on it. She also mentions her career in terms of the more personal goals she has set for it, such as blazing new paths for women. She says that she wants to "make a difference in the world." The writer proves that this is more than just rhetoric by specifying a particular area where she could concentrate her actions. She also mentions philanthropy, a common theme, but proves its validity by demonstrating how she has already begun to commit herself to the cause. What makes this essay strong, then, is not the goals themselves (which are extremely common) but the fact that she makes each one unique by personalizing them through specific examples.

ESSAY 37: Anderson, philanthropy

In thirty to forty years, when you reflect back on your life, what criteria will you use when judging if you have been successful? What are the main achievements/events that you hope will have taken place?

If I can reflect back at my life objectively and feel with certainty that I have been a philanthropist, then I will personally consider my life to be successful. By the word "philanthropist" I mean a true lover of mankind; a positive contributor of all sorts rather than just a monetary donor. We are all mortal, but the effects of our actions are often not. I will consider myself a philanthropist and positive contributor to my community and society if I have continually striven for personal growth, nurtured a positive and loving family, and if I have led and motivated others to also act as philanthropists.

As a true philanthropist, I believe I should donate time, energy, and wisdom to my community as well as money. By growing as a person I can better give of myself. I currently strive for personal growth by building upon my actions to date, by setting short- and long-term goals, and by regularly analyzing my progress through self-analysis and feedback. For example, over the last few years I have certainly grown intellectually; the challenge at this point is to continue. In college, I learned the basics of calculus and physics as a prerequisite to understanding the intricacies of chemical reactions and transport phenomena. Thus, I have slowly improved my understanding of how the physical world works. Simultaneously, I attempted to deepen my understanding of the English language by reading thought-provoking literature and by taking classes such as a creative writing elective and a Works of Shakespeare colloquium.

As a short-term goal, I plan to continue my intellectual growth by learning the basics of economics and finance in order to better understand the intricacies of management and decision sciences. In time, I will correspondingly improve my understanding of how the global marketplace works. As a long-term goal for intellectual growth, I want to become a college professor in twenty-five years, inspiring another generation of young and motivated minds while exposing myself to new concepts and developments. Through goal-setting and continuous feedback, I believe I will continue my intellectual growth. Through an analogous process, I believe I will mature emotionally and improve my physical wellness. As a result, I will be better prepared to give of myself.

Another method I see of becoming a true philanthropist is to nurture a positive and cooperative family. Our children and family members are often our own greatest legacy, adapting to our influences (good or bad) and reflecting them back onto society for years to come. If I should have the opportunity to share in a family of my own (longevity is never guaranteed) then I will commit time and energy to my family, acting in their best interests and treating my children with respect and care as meaningful individuals within our group. By giving freely of myself and by providing a safe and positive environment, I hope that I will be able to leave behind a generation who will pursue their own personal fulfillment, contributing in their own ways.

Finally, through the principle of increasing returns, I can magnify my efforts as a philanthropist by inspiring others to act similarly. Throughout my life, I have held leadership roles in boy scouts, high school clubs, and college activity groups. Currently, I lead as a member of our profit center leadership team, credit union supervisory committee, and employees association board of directors. During college and especially during my three years of work experience, I have been exposed to many different styles of effective and ineffective leadership. Because I have rarely held direct supervisory authority, my leadership has by necessity been performed via personal influence. I convince my coworkers or group members that the goals I am attempting to achieve are worthwhile and obtainable. I provide the means for them to support the goals and then communicate support for their efforts. At times, I gently redirect their efforts. If, in my leadership roles, I have treated my coworkers and group members with respect and provide them with honest feedback, it is likely that they will respond to others in a similar manner. If my leadership experiences are marked by respect and cooperation rather than by jealousy and unhealthy competition, then I will be magnifying my own efforts of being a philanthropist.

In reflection, I will look back on my life thirty or forty years from now and ask myself if I have been a philanthropist. Did I lead a life of contribution, marked by personal growth? Did I nurture a caring and positive family environment? Did I use my leadership to act as a philanthropist and motivate others to act similarly? If, objectively, I can answer "yes" to all of these questions, I will consider my life to be a success.

Comments

This candidate uses the single, broad goal of philanthropy to give meaning and perspective to a number of more specific plans. These include becoming a college professor and raising a family. Giving his essay (and his life) this strong central theme lends nice structure to the essay and sets the impression of a very motivated, focused, and serious individual. He also cleverly incorporates his past academic achievements into the essay by showing them to have been a response to his philanthropic motivations. The essayist could have used a slightly less heavy-handed tone. Applicants are expected to loosen up a bit when answering personal questions, but his essay was deadpan serious. His tone did not hurt him, but being more personable makes even solid, well-done essays more memorable.

Personal Background and Influence

- Clearly explain how you have been affected by your background and influences.

- Be specific in describing how you've been impacted—what have you done differently?

- Describe your unique background but do not include experiences that would make the committee uncomfortable.

This type of question is similar to the role model question. It attempts to learn more about you through the forces that have shaped you. Many applicants mistakenly believe that this is an essay about a trip, a person, or a pastime. They go on at length, describing the influence in detail, without making a connection between it and themselves. The school is not interested in learning more about a dear relative, a memorable holiday, or a motivational book. They are interested in learning more about you. Demonstrate which qualities of the person or experience under discussion have influenced you and in what ways.

What specific aspect(s) of the book, person, or event made an impression on you and how? What action did you take to turn this impression into personal development and change? Did your uncle's willingness to take risks and ability to bounce back from failure inspire you to pick up and move on after a personal setback? Did a trip to a factory in a third-world country cause you to reconsider your position about child labor laws? This is the type of information business schools seek when they ask this question.

A question can be daunting when it asks you to describe your family background. No family is ideal. You need not have had 1.5 siblings, a dog, and a white picket fence in order to write comfortably about your family. In fact, a unique background will set you apart. Still, this is no place to air dirty laundry. If this question has you staring uncomfortably at a blank page, then stop thinking about trying to describe your entire family history in a few paragraphs. Just think of two or three defining moments or interesting incidents. Concentrate on bringing them to life. You will then find that by focusing on the parts, you have painted an accurate picture of the whole.

ESSAY 38: Anderson, typical family background

Please provide us with a summary of your personal and family background. Include information about where you grew up, your parents' occupations, your siblings, and perhaps a highlight or special memory from your youth.

One of the most significant factors that has shaped who I am today is my close-knit family. Born and raised in Los Angeles, I spent a great deal of time during my youth with my relatives because all of them, from grandparents to aunts and uncles to cousins, live in the Los Angeles area. Until the age of twelve, I lived in a comfortable house in Westwood. Residing only a few blocks from UCLA, I remember taking Sunday afternoon walks through the campus and stopping in Westwood Village for a bite to eat. While many M.B.A. candidates apply to Business School with limited knowledge of the campus to which they are applying, I feel fortunate to have been familiar with the many facets of UCLA since my childhood.

One of the most unique aspects of my youth was growing up with a twin sister. My only sibling, Susan epitomized risk-taking and adventure, while I personified hard work and responsibility. Whereas Susan encouraged me to live for the moment and taught me to do my first back flip off of a diving board, I helped her define her goals and persuaded her to set up a savings account. Our distinct personalities balanced each other well, and we have each acquired many of the traits that we admire in the other.

Susan and I attended elementary school together. She continued her education at Los Angeles School followed by college at a U.C. School. I pursued a similar path, attending a private school in Los Angeles, and then doing my undergraduate work at a different U.C. School. Although we attended different schools, Susan and I stayed extremely close and I feel fortunate to have a sister that is also a close friend. While most siblings fight more often than not, Susan and I rarely argued during our childhood, and she always protected me fiercely as her "little sister" even though I am only five minutes younger than she.

My experiences at my high school, a private, all-women high school in Los Angeles, first taught me the intrinsic value of academic achievement. I hold particularly fond memories of the professor of my 7th grade Ancient History class, Dr. Smith. Dr. Smith made learning so exciting and provocative that even the traditionally monotonous memorization of historical names and dates incited intense debates within the class. When Dr. Smith got excited about a subject, he would jump on his desk and stomp his feet to emphasize his points. Through his passion for knowledge, Dr. Smith helped me to realize that academics are not only a practical part of life, but also a challenging and rewarding undertaking that can open doors that are otherwise permanently locked.

My parents have always been an integral part of my life. At the age of twelve, I moved from Westwood to Brentwood where my parents still reside. My adolescence was marked by countless weekends with my family at the beach, playing volleyball and paddle tennis. In addition, my family has always been actively involved in our church. I recall numerous Sunday mornings as a teenager when I could barely drag myself from bed at such an early hour; nevertheless, my parents would always insist that the entire family attend church together. As I look back, I appreciate their persistence, for religion has since become a fulfilling and satisfying part of my life.

My mother, has always served as a model of all that women can achieve in traditionally male-dominated arenas. After receiving her B.A. from a California State University and her M.S.W. from UCLA, she worked in social welfare for several years. In 1984, she founded her own consulting firm. Her firm, of which she is the sole proprietor, provides issues management and consensus planning to many large public and private sector clients nationwide. She has continuously demonstrated not only the benefits of a successful career, but also that talented women can succeed in whatever profession they choose. I took my mother's lead early on and held jobs throughout all of high school and most of college, delighting in the "hands-on" experience I gained.

Having received his B.S. and M.B.A. from the University of Southern California, my father, pursued a career in financial planning. After several years in portfolio management, he began focusing on financial planning for healthcare organizations. He is now a principal of a medical practice management consulting firm that he co-founded. His firm specializes in facilitating healthcare mergers and acquisitions, and in setting up alternative delivery systems throughout the West Coast. Since I am following in my father's footsteps by pursuing a career in the healthcare industry, he is an invaluable mentor and resource.

I am fortunate to have had a gratifying and supportive upbringing. I look forward to building on my excellent education, as I emulate the entrepreneurial successes of my parents. Furthermore, the religious spirit and the sense of community responsibility that my family instilled in me are important components of everything I hope to accomplish.

Comments

This candidate appears to have lived an almost absurdly stereotypical version of the American dream. The merit of this essay, however, is not in its portrayal of personified perfection. The essay's merits come from its excellent organization and writing and from being very personal and warm. You get the sense of a bright, capable, unspoiled woman who has benefited from a stable upbringing and the good influence of a rewarding family life.

ESSAY 39: Stanford, unique family background

Each of us has been influenced by the people, events, and situations occurring in our lives. How have these influences shaped who you are today?

I believe in the adage that we are the sum of our life experiences. I know that my personality, ambition, interests and motivations have been shaped by a specific set of factors: my family, my upbringing in Mississippi, my experiences at Andover and then at Yale and the challenge of my current job. Because I am one of the world's few Catholic, Egyptian Mississippians who went to an Ivy League School, the particular set of influences affecting my development has been distinctive.

I come from a very close and supportive family. They instilled in me many of the values and beliefs that I still hold. My parents, both busy and successful professionals, established their families as their first priority. My mother would often leave her office early to watch her sons' baseball or basketball games. My father, too, was usually home by 5 P.M. in order to help cook dinner in time for us all to get to the evening's event. When work held him at the office late, he would always come home in time to say "good night" to his children before we fell asleep, regardless of the significance of the meeting. My parents taught me the importance of the family as a unit of support and they have provided me with a solid foundation on which to eventually build a family of my own. As an example of the importance of familial ties to me, I have opted to spend 90 percent of my vacation time in Mississippi, instead of more exotic locations, to be with my family.

My father, who is the most ethical person I know, instilled in me a sense of fairness and justice. He is also extremely selfless. As an example, he was involved in politics not for glamour or self-aggrandizement, but because he knew he had the ability and motivation to help people. In addition, I have learned from some of his missteps. His political career ended because he lost a race against an incumbent in his own party who was unpopular but had a large amount of money. While I admired his objectives, I learned the necessity of taking a practical approach to achieving my goals. He might still be in politics and able to help people in that forum, had he delayed running for four years.

From my mother I gained an appreciation of the diverse backgrounds of others and an understanding of their various points of view. She has a sharp intuition and an ability to put herself in others' shoes. I believe that I have inherited both of these qualities. Her ambition has always allowed her to dream for herself and for her children. However, she never stops with a fantasy. She pursues everything she does with a passion. One of the most important lessons she has imparted to me has been that many people live in the past or in the future, but those who are happiest live in the present, enjoying every moment and every stage of their lives.

My parents also taught me the value of education. They lived a Spartan lifestyle in order to send their children to the best schools possible. Because my parents were involved in politics, they read several newspapers religiously. My brother and I became addicted as well, often fighting to get in line for a section we liked. The obsession to read the newspaper daily is a personality quirk that has stayed with me. Wherever I am, I always find a *New York Times* and read it cover to cover. If necessary I collect the papers when I am working 20 hour days and read them at the end of the week. I feel a need to absorb as much information as possible in order to broaden my horizons.

My upbringing in Mississippi has shaped my accepting and sympathetic demeanor towards others. Mississippians are proud people who maintain a close association with and loyalty to their families and communities. Walking along the streets of Jackson, it is customary to smile or say "hi" to almost everyone you pass, and definitely to everyone you make eye contact with. Once our car broke down on the highway in Mississippi and within 10 minutes, five cars had stopped to help us out. Also, growing up in an environment in which poverty was so abundant has had a profound effect on me. It is one of the sources of my mission in life to improve the fortune of others. I believe that there are many ways in which to do that, including building a successful business that creates jobs for people who otherwise would not have been employed.

I was always highly motivated academically, usually ranking first or second in my class. By ninth grade, the lack of challenges and the de-emphasis of academic success in Mississippi's public schools had thoroughly frustrated me. As a result of peer pressure, I was often embarrassed of the national math competitions I would attend. I independently decided to look for opportunities to attend high school elsewhere in order to seek a more challenging environment. I informed my parents and, while they were not anxious for me to leave home at the age of 15, they supported the decision. After visiting several schools, however, I didn't truly feel comfortable at any of them. I had a different accent, different clothes and a different attitude than the other students I met on the tours. I eventually decided that, while the atmosphere intimidated me, the exceptional academic experience would be worth it. Because of all of my reservations, it would have been very easy for me to stay in Jackson. In reality, applying to colleges as a public high school student from Mississippi would have increased my chances of admission. Although there were several points during the first year and one half that I considered leaving, I decided to stay. By the middle of my second year, I had become comfortable in the environment and by senior year I was also more content with myself.

The Andover experience positively influenced the formation of my personality in several ways. First, it significantly broadened my horizons. I began to understand the limitless nature of the opportunities available to me. I met students from other countries, inner cities and divorced families, all of which were completely foreign to me. I started to appreciate both the advantageous aspects of the Mississippi lifestyle and also its substantial limitations. Second, I experienced a transformation in my understanding of my own capabilities. In the first year and one half of classes, I perpetually felt under-prepared. My knowledge base was much less extensive than that of my counterparts who had been educated in urban private schools. My communication skills were also not as well polished. As I worked on improving my own ability to conceptualize and analyze information and my verbal and written communication skills, my self-confidence increased. Partially as a result of graduating with high honors, I left Andover knowing that I have the potential to contribute significantly to society.

At Yale, I developed more fully on a intellectual, social and spiritual levels. The preparation I had received at Andover gave me a significant advantage over others in college. In the classroom, I became a more significant contributor to class discussions than I had previously been. My friends and classmates began to look to me for academic input and advice. I also developed a more enlightened perspective concerning my academic experience. I began to apply the academic frameworks I had learned to more realistic situations and problems. I more fully investigated the public policy and economic implications of the theories. The most significant academic experiences of my four years were the independent research projects which I completed. For one of the first times in my academic career, I was afforded the freedom to dig beneath the surface of an issue, exploring all of the nuances and angles which my mind could devise. My research was praised as insightful, original and thought-provoking. The work propelled my intellectual independence and increased my critical reasoning skills. The holistic perspective I developed also allowed me to view religion and its significance in my life differently. Up until that point, I had blindly followed the religious teachings of the church and my father who is a devout Catholic. At Yale as a result of challenging my religious beliefs, I am now a more faithful, yet less dogmatic, follower.

I have made significant strides in my professional development since joining McKinsey & Co. One of the most challenging aspects of this job is that I am repeatedly placed in a position to talk about high level issues with very senior management. When I started one year ago, I would sit in meetings and only answer questions when asked. Since then, I have developed both a better understanding of business issues and how to solve them and a more refined ability to communicate effectively with senior managers about these topics. As a result, I am now an active participant, and sometimes leader, of high level meetings. My maturation on several fronts has allowed me to become a more effective consultant and to take on more client contact-intensive projects than would normally be expected of an analyst with one year of experience. My improved ability to communicate orally and verbally has helped me build credibility among senior management. As an example of my improved communication skills, I often write my own 20 slide presentations, which are not altered or sometimes even looked at before being presented to the client in update meetings or more informal discussions. Also, my breadth of experience is sometimes more extensive than that of the managers to whom I consult. I can draw parallels to other companies or industries that add value to the current issue by helping to stimulate creative thinking. This skill also helps increase my credibility. I am extremely proud of the progress I have made in terms of my professional development.

In conclusion, I believe that I posses several important qualities that will allow me to contribute to the Stanford community and also to make the most of my Stanford M.B.A.: ambition, self-motivation, concern for others, leadership potential and humor. These qualities are the result of my many diverse experiences, none of which I regret.

Comments

In contrast with the last essay, this candidate has a less typical background than the average candidate and knows how to use it to his benefit. He still stresses all the same qualities that business schools seek ("Ambition, self-motivation, concern for others, leadership potential and humor") but makes each of these qualities come alive through descriptions of his unusual childhood. He even goes so far as to tag himself as, "One of the world's few Catholic, Egyptian Mississippians who went to an Ivy League School." This unique, self-subscribed identity adds color to the rest of his application, shedding light on and giving new dimension to all the accomplishments and achievements found there.

ESSAY 40: Berkeley, father's influence, integrity

What seminal influences or experiences, broadly defined (a book, teacher, friend, relative, sojourn, hobby, and so forth), have especially contributed to your personal development? What correlation, if any, does your personal development have to your professional goals?

Of the many diverse experiences I have had over the last twenty-five years, my father has been and continues to be the most formative influence on my personal development. He has shaped my personality both actively and through example, and can be easily identified by anyone who knows our family well as the source of my strong sense of values and my passion to work with others as a teacher, leader, or team member.

Integrity is one of the tenets of my being; it is the one value that has been instilled in me by my father and strengthened by almost every environment I have come into contact with since I was a young child. My father is the most honest person I know. I have seen his honesty and straightforwardness taken advantage of by others more than once while growing up, to the point where I have even complained that he needed to be more aggressive with the people involved in the situation. His response has always been unwavering, emphasizing that in the long-run the benefits of complete integrity in both business and personal dealings with others will lead to success, while anything less will eventually hinder a person's career. This is advice not easily understood by students and young professionals who find themselves in competitive, pressure filled environments where the drive to "get ahead" is part of everyone's personality. Now that I have competed in the business world, I can fully appreciate the magnitude of my father's professional success and his commitment to integrity. He recently retired at age 49 after 25 years with Colorado's largest private commercial bank holding company, where he started as an Assistant Cashier after graduating from the [large state university] and was most recently Executive V.P. and a member of the Board of Directors. He believes that his integrity and ability to view individual events with a long-term outlook were largely responsible for his career successes, which have provided me with tangible proof that the values I was raised with are the key to my future professional and personal success.

Although my father's influence in shaping who I am has decreased in recent years, my undergraduate education and recent professional experiences have also focused on the importance of key personal values such as integrity. [Ivy league school], as any quality undergraduate experience, goes to considerable lengths to provide a positive learning environment for a talented and diverse group of people. The College Honor Code, which basically entrusts the enforcement of an individual's conduct both inside and outside of the classroom to all students, is tantamount to creating this environment. I found that in addition to functioning well, the system strengthened the values that most students already possessed and instilled a sense of these values in those with less of a focus on ethics. As a young manger in training at GE, C.E.O. Jack Welch's gospel of "GE Values" and "the keys to being a leader" both stressed integrity as number one, ahead of "vision", "accountability and commitment", "empowerment" and "passion for change." "Integrity, Integrity, Integrity" was a familiar phrase among the management ranks at GE—it reminded me of my father. The message was similar when the C.E.O. of [San Francisco investment bank] addressed his new class of forty analysts as follows: "[San Francisco investment bank] is the oldest investment bank in the country", he said, "where others have exercised questionable judgment or behavior in pursuit of a quick buck, [San Francisco investment bank] has focused on long-term relationships and operated with complete integrity". My experience as a corporate finance analyst at [San Francisco investment bank] has borne out the truth that [San Francisco investment bank] is one of, if not the most, conservative underwriters in the U.S. Integrity is more important than ever in the highly regulated, big money world of investment banking because one error in judgment by one employee could, in [San Francisco investment bank]'s case, taint a 195 year history of integrity and impair the future success of the firm.

In addition to a strong sense of values centered around integrity, my father possessed amazing interpersonal and motivational skills. Even as a young child it was apparent to me how much the younger officers at my father's bank respected him. He was a strong leader, as anyone in his position had to be, but he was also modest and team-focused. His encouragement and example helped me to develop my affinity for working in teams and my passion to teach others. I have always found group dynamics and team competition challenging, in both athletics and an academic/professional environment. I spent all four years in College playing varsity volleyball, a sport that, because three of the six players typically touch the ball every time it crosses the net, emphasizes teamwork more than any other I have experienced. The opportunity to captain the team as a senior was a challenging experience that sharpened my leadership skills.

The work environment at [San Francisco investment bank] demands teamwork day in and day out, as the Health Care Corporate Finance Group in San Francisco is comprised of eight professionals including myself. The group's small size means that each individual's performance is very visible to everyone else and the success of the group is inextricably tied to strong contributions from all involved parties. A large part of my success in this very intense environment has been not only my ability to share ideas with and learn from the more senior members of the team, but the ability to operate among professionals who often don't agree with each other and are "stressed out" at times, a skill my father perfected.

My passion to teach others, whether formally or just to help someone with the task at hand, stems from my father's desire to ensure that all of his children learned to appreciate the personal rewards to be gained from teaching and giving. Selfishness was something he would not tolerate. Teaching, although now only a hobby, has always interested me. At [Ivy league school], I "modified" my Economics major to include Education and I spent my off-terms and vacations teaching skiing to children in Vail, Colorado. There is nothing quite like the smile on a twelve year-old's face when they have learned to explore an entire mountain on skis when a week earlier they could not put their equipment on without help. More recently, I taught Junior Achievement to fourth-graders while working at GE. Currently, my desire to teach has been centered on the training of [San Francisco investment bank]'s newest analyst class. The firm has no formalized training program and I have enjoyed teaching merger accounting, financial statement analysis, financial modeling, and other basic survival skills to the bright-eyed recent graduates. This is one of the aspects of my job I find most rewarding.

The development of my strong sense of integrity, ability to both lead and work well in teams, and passion to teach others has convinced me that I have the potential to manage an organization. This is my ultimate professional goal, and it is where I hope to put my fathers influence on my personal development to use professionally. As a corporate leader, I would be required to shoulder the burden of integrity and to motivate and educate others. I believe that my personal development has reached a stage where I am prepared to begin these challenges.

Comments

Many people caution about using a parent as a source of inspiration if the question does not specifically call for it. This essayist proves, however, that any subject can be treated well if done sincerely. He also knows exactly when to step away from the descriptions of his father to bring the focus back to himself. The essayist shows ways in which his father's influence has translated into action and experience, such as his involvement in college team sports and teaching. His concluding paragraph is strong and reemphasizes the three points he has illustrated throughout.

ESSAY 41: Michigan, politics, rock climbing, disability
Describe yourself and the significant events that have shaped you.

Recently, I was trapped on a ledge more than 300 feet above the ground when an unexpected snow storm hit while rock climbing. I was

CHAPTER 14: Getting Personal

stranded until dark and forced to spend the night, unprepared and uncomfortable. The following morning, after a scramble to the top and a
frantic descent, I made an 8:00 A.M. briefing with the Governor, still a bit
disheveled. I was asked afterwards whether I were more proud for having
survived or more embarrassed for having gotten myself into the predicament. My reply characterized much about who I am. I would feel dumb, I
replied, if I were to get myself into the same predicament a second time.
However, I was proud of the fact that I had pushed myself beyond comfortable limits. I look forward to pushing myself hard enough to encounter
many different predicaments in the future.

The mishap occurred in preparation for a larger climb I planned to
undertake several weeks later. Despite the mishap, I continued training
for, and ultimately completed a tower called Independence, a 600-foot
sandstone rock formation that towers over the desert floor of the Colorado National Monument. The tower had come to represent an uncon-
quered challenge throughout my years as an outdoors enthusiast—my
first climb over 500 feet and, to my knowledge, the first ascent by a
climber with only one hand. Despite warnings that I might not be able
to complete the climb, I had undertaken almost eight months of intense
physical training, hours of mental preparation and even a night on a
snow-covered ledge to make the dream possible.

Too often, people talk about what might be, without following
through. I am driven to stretch more than just my imagination. There is
too much to be learned and too much to be overcome, to sit back and
allow opportunities to pass. Although it is hard to pinpoint the source
of who I am, the obstacles I have overcome in my life have made me a
strong, independent and creative person. As I have overcome obstacles
that I was not supposed to, I have developed a confidence and a level of
comfort outside of traditional expectations that very much shape my approach to professional, social and intellectual activities.

In high school, I ran for student body president primarily because no
one else dared run against the popular football team captain. I decided
that precisely because people were afraid to challenge the status quo,
they needed an alternative. Although I was less well known, I ran a campaign and won. That decision had a significant impact on the development of my career. I look back on that somewhat spontaneous decision
as the moment that I consciously realized that the identity we keep and
the context we live within are defined by others only as long as we allow
them to be.

Since then, I can name many similar examples that have helped
embed a tremendous sense of personal confidence in listening to my
heart rather than someone else's discouragement. I taught myself to
play tight end and made the high school football team as a walk-on
without any prior experience. I was selected as the youngest member of

the U.S. Disabled Ski Team after organizing my own run-a-thon to raise funds for the flight to a qualifying race in Italy.

In college, I chose to carry a minor in African American studies in addition to my double major in economics and political science, even though the minor was not required. I also wrote a thesis, which was optional, and I earned a $1000 grant from the school to carry out research on low income community development in Oakland, California. I wanted to do more than just get by. I chose to go beyond college requirements to complete the work I felt necessary to do justice to my academic interests.

I have realized that I can be a much deeper person if I take the initiative to do so. Whereas most of my college counterparts completed majors in order to "get through," I turned my four years at Colorado College into a deeply focused study of the economic, political and social underpinnings of social inequality in this country. I chose to expand my studies to enrich my understanding and I chose to study in Oakland to apply some of my ideas and test my assumptions.

In the Governor's office, I have assumed substantial responsibility for my age—in large part because I have taken the initiative to do so. Despite frequently encountering skepticism about whether I am old enough for the job, I have earned the trust of the governor through my own effort and persistence.

I have developed a great breadth of interests and studies. Sometimes to my own detriment, however, I feel driven to explore too many challenges and to take advantage of too many new opportunities. This occasionally leads to a sense of being scattered or too thinly spread. It leads me to sometimes awkwardly balancing a number of different worlds rather than just focusing on one. I find myself trying out for the annual college dance performance just because I've never done modern dance before while also trying to keep up with my reading for a political theory discussion group. I find myself volunteering my time for others when I can hardly find time for my studies. I find myself organizing a one-mile, running race for charity through the campus library while trying to balance work and responsibilities as student body president.

Today, I am no better. I am carrying extensive professional responsibility, but still teaching myself guitar after midnight, exploring opportunities for founding a magazine about responsible corporate citizenship and helping students at my alma mater organize a campaign to challenge the administration on its quality standards for teaching on campus.

For all the scattering, however, I have managed to be successful at most of what I take on. This is because I am scattered by choice. This spread of activity has taught me to carry substantial responsibility and not to shy away from challenging opportunities. Often the difference between a good idea and a fantasy is whether someone seizes upon the opportunity to make it happen. I have taught myself to balance a variety of interests and to appreciate a range of perspectives. This makes me a stronger policy maker, a better student and a deeper person. These are skills are experiences that will be invaluable to me throughout my career.

Comments

The essayist wrote a great first line. This candidate tackles quite a broad range of subjects, which (case in point) does not always weaken the essay. He even tackles the subject of having too many projects and commitments, which he calls "being scattered." He gets away with it because he is truly accomplished in many of these areas and has made lifelong commitments to some. This would be a harder angle for someone to take if that person never followed through on any of the activities in which he or she dabbled. The writer also makes nice use of colorful details (from trying out for a modern dance performance to organizing a one-mile charity running race) to bring himself alive to the readers.

ESSAY 42: Stanford, influence of relationships
What matters most to you, and why?

Living in midtown Manhattan during the terrorist attacks and being a colleague of many of the victims, forced a period of personal reflection. The conclusion? The people who are a part of my life should be valued above everything else.

Small Towns and Relationships

I left my friends, family, and fiancée, to move from Kansas City to New York City to pursue my career. Until that point, I had lived my entire life in Kansas, the majority of it on a farm in a rural area. In fact, my modest apartment building today in NYC has more occupants than the entire high school from which I graduated. My small town background taught me many important, though often unspoken, lessons for living a fulfilling life. The most important lesson I have recently revisited is that close relationships enhance happiness. Unfortunately, I did not fully appreciate this message until the terrorists' attacks demonstrated how life cannot be taken for granted. The calls, e-mails and prayers I received immediately following the disaster were incredibly touching. Family, friends, fraternity brothers, and even high school classmates I had not seen in years all seemed to be in contact. Since relationships are fundamentally important to me, I will use this time to discuss those individuals who had the greatest impact on my development and who matter the most to me.

My Grandparents

My grandparents were perhaps the most sincere, kindest people I know. Our relationship developed when I was a child as they would look after me for half-days during my kindergarten year. Each day together, we would split our time between doing chores and fun activities. My grandparents were so happy and full of life that I was naturally drawn to them and gladly contributed to work around the farm. For a five-year-old to be willing to forgo playing games to help with chores, you can imagine their gift with people. We also enjoyed our share of laughter and fun activities. My grandmother is famous for telling me that "we have to work-a-little and play-a-little." I still think of her and that saying every time I plan my activities for the upcoming week and always include time to catch a good college basketball game or dinner with friends amid my busy work schedule.

Both of my grandparents spent almost their entire lives on a farm. However, they were also the first within my family to attend college. They began the family legacy at the University of Kansas, which my father, aunts, uncles, cousins, brother and I gladly followed. I hope someday that my children will be the fourth generation representing our family at the University and will carry on our family's proud tradition.

My Parents

My parents, both health care professionals, left a farm life to pursue higher education degrees, only to return to Kansas years later to start our family. Learning, hard work, and their children's athletic pursuits were the cornerstone of our household values.

My father, a physician, is a quiet, intellectual, and inspiring person. He followed his dream of becoming a doctor and completed 14 years of post-secondary education to achieve it. I inherited his athletic abilities, quantitative nature, and kind heart. In fact, many of my fondest childhood memories revolve around sports. He would rebound for hours as I imitated my favorite college and NBA heroes shooting thousands of baskets on hot, Kansas, summer nights. Even during my teenage years, we could always communicate about sports.

My mother is more artistic than athletic. Thus, she worked hard to broaden my horizon beyond sports, introducing me to her passions: painting and reading. Though I never developed her touch with a paintbrush, I developed a love of reading, and the town librarian knew us very well. Since we lived miles from town and my mother worked part-time, we spent many hours together. Through conversations, games, and work she never missed an opportunity to praise and encourage me. The self-confidence she instilled in me gave me the courage to aggressively pursue my dream of a Wall Street career.

My Brother

My older brother is a computer programmer, collegiate football player, and entrepreneur at heart. He is nine years my senior and the best man in my upcoming wedding. Our age disparity permitted us to avoid typical sibling rivalry and allowed me to truly admire my brother. We are identical in neither stature nor skill set, but I believe this is why I admire him so.

[Brother's Name] does everything big. At last count, he has started 7 businesses. His most recent venture, begun while he completed his M.B.A. degree, developed into a multi-million dollar manufacturing company, which continues to acquire its competitors. [Brother's Name] is a strategic thinker, keen at spotting opportunity and has been a strong advocate of an M.B.A. for my career progression. However, from all of these wonderful things, my brother is also consistently tardy.

From my relationship with my brother, I developed two traits: 1) An entrepreneurial spirit, and 2) A firm respect for other people's time. Simply by watching [Brother's Name] develop his ideas from vision into reality, I could feel the excitement. My search for the satisfaction of being self-employed led me to start two small businesses of my own. The first, a lawn mowing company, brought me steady, if not substantial, spending money through high school and my first years of college. The second, a real estate business, taught me more but is less successful financially. In real estate, I created an L.L.C. to buy and rent single family homes. However, through this enterprise I have learned the challenges that come with being an out-of-state landlord. Finally, the time issue. After consistently waiting on [Brother's Name] for various activities throughout the years, I vowed that I would never start a meeting (personal or professional) with the other party frustrated at my tardiness. The consequences are potentially too great. I now insist on arriving early to all meetings and appointments, and do not take pleasure in arriving "fashionably" late.

My Good Friend

My lifelong friend is a former teammate and social butterfly. We grew up together and were inseparable. We learned many life-lessons at an early age playing soccer, baseball, football, and tennis together. We learned how teamwork, preparation, and emotions can influence the outcome of a game. Even today as my research team competes against rival firms, these lessons are applicable to our efforts. Often our key information is gathered from colleagues, our best written material produced after countless rewrites, and most successful stock recommendations given based on facts, not emotion. He and I have not lived in the same town for eight years, but still visit almost daily. I know our relationship will endure for a lifetime.

My Fiancée

My fiancée, and new best friend. She has been a source of encouragement, strength, and spirit since our relationship began during our undergraduate education. We challenge each other to pursue our individual dreams and support each other in these endeavors. However, due to our career pursuits, we have been separated geographically for almost two years. Not being together for all of the daily triumphs that many others take for granted is a sacrifice that has required great resolve and taught us valuable lessons about communication. Through this time I have become much more aware of communication styles. For instance, [Fiancée's name] typically displays her emotions in her body language. Thus, without seeing her, I have learned to be more cognizant of her tone and word selection. At the same time, I consciously try to capture more details of my personal experiences to share, since she cannot be present to experience them firsthand. As a result, both my awareness of others and verbal and written communication has improved significantly during our time apart.

The special people described above, and the talents and virtues of each, have helped define what matters most to me today. I am a balance of all of these people with a few quirks thrown in. The sum is a person with just a piece of my good friend's blatant assertiveness, a lot of my father's reserved demeanor, much of my brother's competitive spirit and confidence to dream big, more and more of my fiancée's passion and nonjudgmental heart, all of my mother's love of reading and enjoyment of new experiences, a great deal of my grandfather's work ethic and loyalty, and nearly all of my grandmother's positive spirit and political conservatism. And fortunately for me, they all love me unconditionally and are the core support group that will provide me the strength and confidence to continue to pursue my dreams, including a Stanford M.B.A.

Comments

This is a strong essay because the author lets his guard down. He gets very personal and allows the committee to see him as a compassionate and thoughtful individual who cares deeply about those close to him. He relies only on his personal relationships as influence but is concrete in how each has impacted him. From his grandparents he learned to balance work with fun; from his parents he developed a love of sports and reading; his brother peaked his entrepreneurial spirit and a respect for others' time; his best friend gave him an appreciation for teamwork; and through his relationship with his fiancée he honed his communication skills. Through the essay, he reveals these positive qualities while proving a respect for and an ability to learn and grow from those around him.

CHAPTER 15

Changes and Challenges

(Technology, International Experience, and Teamwork)

- Responses should demonstrate an ability to adapt to change and rise to challenges.

- Use examples from your past to support your stated abilities.

- Focus on your actions and not the specific situations.

"Times, they are a changing," sings Bob Dylan. You might be thinking that this phrase applies to just about anything but business school applications. However, if you look closely, you will see evidence that today's business schools have indeed kept up with recent trends and revolutions in the workplace. Change itself, for example, now permeates every facet of business. It can occur in reaction to technological developments, be the latest management ideology, or result from your own volition. Also, developments in technology have allowed for increased globalization, which translates into a need for business persons skilled in cross-cultural interaction. Finally, the last decade has seen a renewed focus on the importance of teamwork in organizations. If one of the questions asks about your aptitude in any of these areas, look below for strategies and samples about how to tackle them appropriately.

Change and Technology

- Specific technological skills do not have to be showcased here.

- Provide evidence of your willingness to educate yourself to emerging technologies.

- Demonstrate an ability to manage the integration of new technology.

A person can no longer expect to be in the same career for ten years at a time let alone for a lifetime. Even if you do stay in the same career, you are going to have to deal with change on one level or another. You may implement it yourself or simply try to keep up with it. Your ability to adapt to and even flourish in the volatile atmosphere that permeates today's business world will be vitally important to your success.

Not everyone, however, has reached a high level of comfort with the constantly shifting landscape. If change is not your strong point, then do not try to force it or fake it. Think of a creative way to approach the question instead. Perhaps highlight your ability to lead employees steadily through periods of change by using your stabilizing influence.

Likewise, do not be intimidated by the questions about technological change. The admissions committee is more interested in seeing your common sense approach than your vast knowledge of back-end database technologies. They will not expect you, a future business manager, to understand every detail of the technologies you implement. However, they will expect you to have a broad enough understanding to enable you to make educated decisions. Show the committee that as a manager, you will not shy away from technological change. Prove that you are aware of the importance of keeping educated and abreast of new developments and that this awareness gives you the confidence to make wise technological decisions.

ESSAY 43: Wharton, consulting, team leader
Write about a time when you have experienced change in an organization. Identify and evaluate your role in the process.

In the aftermath of a major strategy study, I had been assigned the task to lead a team through the final detailing and implementation of the company's approach to a nascent high tech market with huge growth potential. It turned out that my team members represented three different business units with completely contradictory ideas and agendas concerning the market in question aiming at their BU's best benefit. My task was to effect the obviously needed change: align all resources towards the best benefit for the company as a whole rather than its BU's. It did not make my job easier that the team was not only cross-BU, but also cross-culture: One French, one British, one German and one Dutch team member.

How did I handle this situation? I concentrated on the classical role of the catalyst. I kept strictly neutral and fact-driven throughout the whole process. I led heated debates back to the factual basis as fast as possible. I emphasized facts, facts and again facts, and made the team collect as many of them as possible in order to minimize the weight of opinions in the discussions.

But that was not enough. Often team members would accuse each other of inventing facts to support their hidden agendas; they would react in an extremely sensitive way to careless as well as carefully crafted political remarks from other team members; they would routinely use their informal network to apply pressure to other team members.

To prevent the team from falling apart, I spent numerous hours with team members individually, visiting them on their "home turf" and experiencing the pressure their colleagues put on them to get the desired results out of my team. In terms of factual content, most of these meetings did not add anything; but they helped defuse the political tension and kept the team going.

After four months, my perseverance began to pay off, and the (Big Consulting Company) approach of "discovered logic" started to show some effect. Pressed by the logic the team's own fact collection and analysis had created positions began slowly to become flexible. Commonalities were discovered, and the idea to serve the benefit of the company as a whole slowly matured from pure lip service into something more substantial.

After six months, the team managed to agree on one single presentation to the board of management. This presentation was extremely successful and fortunately all BU bosses were forced to commit to the approach outlined in that same meeting, some of them more grudgingly than convinced. At least one common approach was agreed upon; whether all BU bosses will wholeheartedly support its implementation or whether some will resort to using their snipers, remains to be seen.

How would I evaluate my performance in this project? I believe I achieved some 80 percent of the change in attitude that was possible in that organization and the given time frame. I paid dearly for that in working hours and physical and psychological stress. But I also learned a lot about human nature, and I came to accept politics as an unavoidable by-product of that nature.

Comments

This essay gives a very real and convincing account of change in the workplace. Inexperienced managers often have very ambitious and naive goals based on their studied perceptions of the big picture. Experience provides a realistic sense of the enormous number of details and loose ends that must be explored and tied up before real change can take effect. This candidate shows that through this experience, he can now appreciate the real effort that goes into effecting change. He also makes good use of a single example and does not try to accomplish too much in one essay.

ESSAY 44: Sloan, nontechnical

Discuss your views regarding the management of technological change as a vital skill for future managers, what impact technological change has had on your chosen career field, and how study at MIT will prepare you to face these challenges.

When I was in junior high my mother, a computer engineer, had on her desk a cutting edge, top-of-the-line calculator. It was a Texas Instruments the size of a cigar box and about as robust in providing quick, easy mathematical solutions. What a difference a decade makes! These days, you can't swing a cat without activating somebody's Web site. Information flows around us in an ever-widening river of digitized words, pictures, and sounds. My friend in Korea can send me electronic letters that arrive instantly. My company, a small mail order firm, can process and precisely track over 1,500 orders a day because of the hardware and software available to us.

The increasing ubiquity of computers has done more than make Bill Gates the world's richest college dropout—it has affected how the managers of tomorrow's corporations must look at information technology. It is obvious these days that to ignore the need for a technological strategy, one that fully integrates with and supports larger corporate objectives, is to commit slow suicide. In a time of rapid change, when machines that are cutting edge today may be obsolete tomorrow, managers must equip themselves with the tools necessary to create a technological strategy that can ride the waves. Long-term thinking requires knowledge of where technology has been, where it is going, and where it can take you. Managers must be on the alert for the trends that will make their businesses more effective and more efficient, while learning to identify and avoid technologies that promise big results but will only deliver big headaches.

The impact of technology has affected every industry, from the largest to the smallest. With a permanent workforce of just 13 people and temp seasonal staff of no more than 10, my company this year processed over 60,000 orders in a 3 month period. Cheaper, faster, smarter computers have lowered barriers to entry in mail order, making it possible for direct mail companies to start up with a minimum of capital and to have more control over the operations of their businesses. While the majority of mail order software, for instance, used to require UNIX or mainframe platforms and tens of thousands of dollars, these days the demand from smaller catalogers for P.C.-based software is being met by a variety of companies. Technology is vital to providing an ideal buying experience for today's direct consumer—from telecommunications systems that queue up callers and provide reports to databases that aid in capturing and analyzing current data and forecasting the future.

MIT has always been a leader in producing technological change, so it makes sense that the Sloan School is tops in producing managers uniquely qualified to understand and deal with that change. During my time with my company I have worn many, many hats, but the work I have found the most intriguing, the most stimulating, has been in operations and MIS. I love to design spreadsheets, to juggle the set-up of our contact manager to make it more effective, and to sit down with new software to figure out how it works and how to tie it in with our existing programs. But for all the fun that I have, I often find myself hitting the limits of my expertise and thinking, I know there's a better way to do this, I just don't know what it is. I feel like I am nibbling at the edges of a vast buffet of knowledge and possibility. At Sloan I hope to fill my plate. I'm ready to gain more depth in my areas of interest, and to exchange ideas in a climate of bracing intellectual vigor. I want to move to the next level, and I believe that Sloan is the vehicle that can take me there.

Comments

This essayist proves that you do not have to understand every detail about technology to write a good essay about technological change. She tackles the subject with confidence. The writer proves that though she may not be a computer programmer, neither is she intimidated by computers, their uses, and their potential. Best of all, she accomplishes this with humor, wit, and a light, easy manner.

ESSAY 45: Sloan, technical

Discuss your views regarding the management of technological change as a vital skill for future managers, what impact technological change has had on your chosen career field, and how study at MIT will prepare you to face these challenges.

Technological innovation is occurring at an ever-increasing pace. In the future, a company's ability to establish, maintain, and increase its competitive advantage over others in its industry will be closely tied to that company's ability to effectively apply technological innovation to improve its operation. The ability of a company to implement change driven by technological innovation, in turn, is dependent upon the ability of its managers to understand the full implications of the technology on the operation of their company. This is indeed a vital skill for future managers in any and every industry. To an even greater extent, managers in industries which are directly tied to technology (e.g., manufacturing) must have a thorough grasp of technology's role in every facet of the operation of their firms. It is this belief that has led me to pursue my graduate education in both engineering and management in order to eventually pursue a career in manufacturing.

In my current position, I have been directly involved in applying technological innovation to increase the efficiency of nuclear power plants. My current career field is engineering consulting to the power generation industry and the U.S. Navy. My firm is involved in a project to introduce a state-of-the-art ultrasonic flow measurement system to measure feedwater flow rates in nuclear power plants. (Feedwater flow is the flow of water that feeds the nuclear reactor. This water is turned to steam, which then feeds turbine generators to produce electricity.) The improved accuracy of this flow measurement technology over conventional methods is used as the basis for increasing feedwater flow rates and thereby boosting the production of electricity. This translates into hundreds of thousands of dollars in additional annual revenue for the utility.

This project is representative of the way in which the nuclear power industry is embracing technological change as it relates to digital instrumentation and controls. Implementing technological change in the nuclear industry is often an uphill battle for two main reasons. The first is the inertia associated with the regulatory constraints within which nuclear utilities must operate. The second is a fundamental distrust of new technologies on the part of many plant managers. This distrust is fueled primarily by a lack of understanding of the technology and has led some managers to dismiss promising technologies before giving them a fair evaluation.

With these insights and experiences in dealing with technological change, I wish to expand my technical and management skills through formal training, and MIT is the ideal place to accomplish this. MIT is at the forefront both in developing new technologies which will have far reaching implications for all industries and in training managers who will have the technical sophistication to make good decisions in implementing technological innovation. The MIT Leaders for Manufacturing Program to which I am applying recognizes the importance of integrating both technical and management skills in order to provide leadership in the field of manufacturing. MIT would help prepare me to face the day-to-day challenges of managing technological change by expanding my knowledge of state-of-the-art manufacturing technologies and expanding my knowledge of the means to bring about technological change in a manufacturing company. Finally, attending a management school within an institution dedicated to the advancement of technology presents two important benefits related to the Institute's close ties to industry. The close ties to industry help ensure that the Sloan curriculum stays focused and relevant to the changing needs of industry. This relationship also presents the potential for active dialogue with manufacturing companies regarding major technological issues confronting the manufacturing sector today.

Comments

As a nuclear power engineer, this essayist is able to tell the committee about a field which they do not usually hear about. He was wise to have described his current project in laymen's terms. Getting too technical, even in response to a technically focused question, results in dry essays that are a bore to read. While this essay is on the dry side, it is accessible enough to read easily. His specifically stated, targeted goals make a good impression.

International Experience

- Demonstrate an open mind and an appreciation for globalization.

- Non-business related international experiences are relevant.

Business schools have not fallen behind the worldwide globalization trend. These questions, uncommon on most business school applications a few years ago, now occur fairly commonly. With increasingly international curricula the top schools are looking for more international experience and exposure from their applicants. An essay that clearly identifies some of the reasons why today's manager must develop a global business perspective and that demonstrates how you have a good head start will prove very effective.

If you have extensive international experience or an unusual ethnic or national background, use this to its full advantage. These details will go a long way in differentiating you from the crowd. If you are not privileged enough to have this type of background, be creative with the experience you do have. Perhaps you have foreign language skills or international business experience on which you can capitalize. Showcase your knowledge of your industry and of current trends by expressing your enthusiasm for globalization and the opportunities that it will open up in your field.

ESSAY 46: Lauder (Wharton), volunteer teacher in Thailand

Tell us about a cross-cultural experience that challenged you. How did you meet this challenge, and what did you learn from the experience?

My most important cross-cultural experience is related to the fifteen months I spent in Thailand as a teacher of Economics and Business in a Cambodian refugee camp.

My admission to ESSEC can be considered a relatively conventional success, a classical way to pursue high quality management studies. After graduating, I decided to go to Thailand to volunteer for a not-for-profit organization. I was satisfied with my academic performance, but I was somehow disappointed by the conventional nature and lack of imagination of the career options available upon graduation. Most of my peers would follow the same path as their predecessors, working as soon as possible for major companies or consulting groups. I felt I should develop my entrepreneurial skills, and diversify my experiences. I thought that I needed above all to follow my personal convictions, give time to others, and pursue my needs for personal discovery.

With the help of a journalist, I was given the opportunity to teach management in a Cambodian refugee camp in Thailand. That man, Mr. DENOIX, was also the director of a small agency called "Agir pour le Cambodge" ("Act for Cambodia"). He helped carry out that personal project I had had in mind for a long time. I arrived in Thailand in September 1989, having left France a bit anxious, but very motivated and enthusiastic. Nevertheless, my idealism regarding the real situation in the refugee camp on the Khmer border was about to be corrected, and I discovered a situation much more complicated and ambiguous than I could have imagined.

"Agir pour le Cambodge" ("Act for Cambodia") is a small Not-For-Profit Organization created in the mid 80's to help the hundreds of thousands of Cambodian refugees who were escaping from both the Khmer Rouge dictatorship and the Vietnamese invasion. The Thai government accepted, under the responsibility of the United Nations Border Relief Operations, to receive these people on its territory, on the condition that no refugee could leave these camps. Very quickly, the main camp ("Site 2") where I taught, became the area with the biggest concentration of Khmer people (over 300 000 refugees) outside of the Cambodian capital Phnom Penh. It was a huge city, in need of a strict organization, and where various humanitarian organizations quickly set up aid programs: hospitals, schools, and so on. . . . I took part in a teaching project initiated by "Agir pour le Cambodge": the Institute of Public Administration. This was a undergraduate school designed to train future Cambodian entrepreneurs and government officials. After two decades of civil war, the country's intellectual class had been decimated . . . .

I was responsible for the Business and Economics Departments, and taught to approximately 300 students. As a teacher of Business, I had different age groups of pupils, from 18 to 50 years old. I taught mainly in English with the younger classes, and sometimes in French or English with a Khmer translator for the older generations. My biggest classes had 180 students, but the normal size was about 30. My teaching had to be adapted to local circumstances, and above all to the particularly tough historical background of the population. Many of the younger pupils were born during the war, had lost part of their family in the tragedy, and had never worked or even experienced the life of a "normal" economic society. In addition, the level of the students within the same class was very unequal. I developed the method of practical case study, taking as often as possible examples from the camp economic life.

I came back from Thailand transformed. More mature and self-confident, I had considerably developed my adaptability, autonomy, and of knowledge of managing people. My responsibilities there were quite significant. The efficiency of my teaching and my way of managing the school and the team of teachers partially determined the future of students. Some of them could obtain grants to study abroad—which meant freedom to them—while others, through a good understanding of business, could earn their livings when they returned, once the UN aid stopped. Moreover, my Thai experience was really difficult. My freedom there had a strange taste. While my students and friends could never leave the camp, we, the foreigners, were not allowed to stay in the camp at night and after curfew. I felt particularly powerless when, during class, the announcement of an imminent bombing was made, and all the foreigners were immediately evacuated to the nearest village, while my Cambodian friends had to stay. It is this experience of war, and my sudden awareness of my privileges which shaped me the most. I will also never forget the friends I made inside the camp, with whom I had some of the deepest relationships I ever established.

I was often criticized for wasting time on such an experience, at a time when people were anxious to continue studies or launch a high-powered career immediately following graduation. I am firmly opposed to that vision of life. I believe that a real manager has a diverse personality, and proves his ability to manage different kinds of situations, in different environments. I felt the need to shape my personality in a different manner, and was never satisfied to follow in the tracks of others. I want to be someone who has both a vast technical knowledge and a good perception of human relationships. Some people tend to forget this second aspect. My experience in Thailand was, in that sense, the most valuable contribution to the strengthening of my personality.

Comments

This candidate benefits enormously from having had such an amazing cultural experience. Moreover, he knows how to use the experience to his best advantage by cushioning his attributes and achievements in the context of an interesting and touching story.

Teamwork

- Effective team participation is important—being team leader is not necessary.

- Team experiences from areas outside of work are just as relevant.

- Focus on your positive contributions—do not linger on conflicts.

Teamwork has always been important to success in the business world. Only lately have people been openly aware and acknowledged it as one of the primary skills sought in a leader. These questions lend credence to the importance of developing group skills and being a team player. Whether you have been the active team member of a focus group, participated in a team sport, or led a group in pursuit of an activity or goal, show how the group has benefited from your involvement. Any situation that shows your positive interaction with others and your ability to motivate and support the people with whom you work should become the focus. Applicants often draw examples from sports and work, but think broadly—teams are everywhere. Your volunteer activities, your church group, your sorority or fraternity, your book club, your political involvement— even your family—all provide good context for positioning yourself as a team player or leader. Show how you helped take a leadership position by motivating the team to further action. Or, take the opposite approach, and show that you know when to step back and swallow your pride for the betterment of the group. When possible, give tangible results.

ESSAY 47: Fuqua, nonprofit team experience

Tell us about the most challenging team experience you have had to date. What role did you play? What factors made it a challenge for you? How did the group address these issues?

After graduation, an opportunity arose for three friends and me to assume significant roles with the Atlanta Clothing Bank Network (ACBN). The ACBN, a local 501(c)3 non-profit organization, collected donations of new clothing from apparel manufacturers, distributors, and retailers, and distributed the clothes to metro Atlanta homeless shelters and halfway houses. In its 3rd year, the ACBN had established an impressive track record by distributing over a half of a million dollars of clothing, but the organization itself was badly floundering. The original founders had moved on in their careers, had started families, or had just burned out. The bookkeeping and finances were in shambles. Donations were lagging. Reviving the ACBN was a daunting task, but three other community-oriented Virginia alumni and I teamed up and offered to take over the ACBN. The founders gratefully accepted.

We divided the responsibilities into Operations, Donor/Client Development, Grant Development, and Executive Director. For the first year, I handled Operations, which included managing the inventory, reconstructing the finances, and filing the taxes. For the second year, I served as Executive Director, representing the ACBN to the community and to potential donors. Over this two year period, the ACBN successfully distributed another half million dollars of clothing. Although we continued to collect and distribute donations, operational funding remained an ongoing challenge. In addition, the administrative burden of running a 501(c)3 corporation distracted the team from developing the ACBN. After two years, the financial challenges and the administrative burden of a 501(c)3 corporation combined to push the other board members and me towards burnout. At the same time, each of us started taking on additional responsibility in our careers in investment banking, commercial banking, and consulting. Our lack of diversity became our Achilles' Heel. To compensate, we shifted responsibilities and sought additional volunteers. We soon realized that unless we hired a paid administrator, the ACBN would never receive the continuous administrative dedication it required; however, our already meager financial support stipulated non-wage activities only. Nonetheless, we continued to seek volunteers and distribute donations as best we could.

Then we received the final blow. The ACBN's warehouse, an unmarked building in a rough section of downtown Atlanta, was burglarized and looted. After sifting through the mess, the loss totaled 90 percent of the inventory. The building itself was insured, but because the value of the donations was arbitrary, our inventory was not. All the hard work went down the drain, and at a time when we had neither the time nor the energy to resurrect the ACBN. Again, our lack of diversity was our Achilles Heel. The current warehouse was slated for demolition with the upcoming Olympics. Also due to the Olympics, similar space was priced well out of our means. With empty coffers, an empty warehouse, and empty hearts, we grudgingly voted to go inactive. We donated the salvageable inventory and materials to the Salvation Army, and closed the doors.

Although we did keep the doors open for two more years and made a difference in the Atlanta community, in retrospect, we see that four optimistic college grads from similar backgrounds and at similar points in their careers were ill-equipped to run an all-volunteer corporation. We lacked the tools, the volunteer experience, the time, and the diversity to take the ACBN to the next level. Although the failure of the ACBN tempered our generally unfaltering optimism, the experience of running a 501(c)3 corporation was an invaluable personal, professional and educational experience for all of us. Our team learned much about running a business, the challenges of non-profit management, and the importance of diversity. I view the resurrection and subsequent failure of the Atlanta Clothing Bank as both the most frustrating and the most educational team experiences I have had. Going forward, the ACBN experience has sensitized me to the importance of diversity on any team, professional or otherwise.

Comments

This is an interesting case of someone using a failed team experience to demonstrate lessons learned. The fact that the project went under is inconsequential. Applicants should not shy away from this kind of example, as long as it answers the question and translates into tangible experience. This candidate, for example, learned firsthand about inventory, finances, taxes, and leadership. To strengthen the essay, he could have shown exactly how the group's lack of diversity negatively affected the situation. He makes the point often but could have drawn the line connecting the two more clearly.

ESSAY 48: Sloan, church team experience

Describe a situation in which you influenced others in an organization. Comment on the professional and/or personal attributes you used to do that and how these attributes might be important to attaining your career goals. How do you expect the Sloan School to further the development of these attributes?

Six months ago, my church implemented a new organizational structure in which all the various church functions were consolidated under the responsibility of one of ten different committees.

I was asked to chair one of the new committees tasked with increasing the level of communication among the various ministry groups in the church. Soon after accepting the position, I expanded the scope of the committee's responsibilities to include maintenance of the church's audiovisual and lighting equipment. This particular church function had not been assigned to any of the newly formed committees, even though it was important to the efficient operation of the church.

The church media department which I undertook to organize would be responsible for operating the various audiovisual and lighting equipment during all church functions ranging from weekly Sunday service to special concerts. My effort in establishing and managing the new media department illustrates how I have been able to influence others in my church to bring about an organizational improvement.

In the initial phase of my effort to establish the department, I had to recruit and train a team of volunteers to operate the various equipment. This was a challenging task which required me to employ a number of different skills. First of all, the task required me to develop and exercise strong persuasion skills to successfully recruit volunteers, some of whom were reluctant to take on the responsibility. Also, during the recruiting phase of my effort, I had to seek out those individuals whom I felt would be best suited to this type of service. This required me to exercise skills in gauging the aptitude and affinity of potential recruits for such work. Since recruiting my team of five volunteer, I have been challenged with maintaining the level of productivity and enthusiasm among the team members for the service they provide to the church community.

I have found that motivating a team of volunteers can be considerably more difficult than motivating a team of paid workers since paid workers usually have certain motivational factors not present in a volunteer organization. Therefore, I have found it necessary to communicate regularly with the individual team members to ensure that they are content with their roles and reminded of the important functions they perform.

The team-building skills I described above which were important in establishing my church's media department are skills which will be important to the attainment of my long-term career goal of managing production operations for a high technology manufacturing firm. In high technology manufacturing industries of the future, managers must be agents of technological change to ensure the success of their companies. The success of implementing change is contingent upon others up and down the ranks of the organization also catching the same vision for change. An effective manager is only able to accomplish this by fostering unity and teamwork. Therefore, good team-building skills are essential.

Sloan is the perfect place to further develop these team-building skills. Sloan's strong collaborative environment provides seemingly unlimited opportunities for team interaction from study groups to various extracurricular activities. As further evidence of Sloan's emphasis on teamwork is the Project TEAM initiative. While other aspects of the Sloan program are indicative of the high regard Sloan as an institution places upon teamwork, the Project TEAM initiative is a clear indication that Sloan students themselves wholeheartedly embrace a strong team-oriented philosophy, as well.

Comments

The applicant wrote a nice example, demonstrating many of the team-building qualities that admissions committees like to see. These include initiative, leadership, motivation, and an active community spirit. He then takes it all one step further in the last paragraph by detailing exactly where, at Sloan, he can put these skills to use.

CHAPTER 16

Miscellaneous

(Explanations, Reapplications, and Other Open-Ended Questions)

- Explanations should be positive if possible—never make excuses.

- If applying for the 2nd time, note what has changed since your previous application.

- Utilize other open-ended questions to present information that would strengthen your position and that you have not yet had the opportunity to share.

You might wish to communicate a particular point about yourself somewhere on your application. However, you may not be sure exactly how or where to communicate it. You may be reapplying and want to address your case in light of your former rejection or acceptance. Perhaps your transcript contains a red flag such as a bad grade or a yearlong hiatus that you would like to explain. You might have a disability or other extenuating circumstances that will shed light on all your other activities. These essays are a good place to accomplish all of these goals. Look at the questions before you begin, and strategize ahead of time. Do not belabor any of the above points. A simple mention or quick explanation of them should be plenty, no matter what the context.

You can tie up any loose ends such as these when answering the optional or open questions, usually the last question asked on any application. These questions are optional only in the technical sense of the word. Even if you do not have any particular circumstance to explain, do not skip any opportunity to move beyond the confines of the previous questions to let the committee members know who you are. Surely you can include more information to strengthen your case. Seize the chance to show the admissions committee that you are a complex and intriguing person by revealing an entirely different side of your personality. You can also simply underscore strengths you only touched on elsewhere in the application.

The following essays show how several applicants have successfully accomplished all of the above.

Explanations

ESSAY 49: Harvard, explaining poor grades

Do you feel your academic history is indicative of your ability to succeed at Harvard Business School? Why or why not? If not, please support with additional evidence of your academic ability.

I believe that my academic record may serve as an indicator of my ability to succeed at Harvard Business School. My university grades and career show a general trend of improvement, and also reflect an ability to understand that there is more to an education than what occurs in the classroom or what is shown on an exam. I feel that my record demonstrates a penchant for academic success at crucial instances, and a generally high level of academic performance throughout my university career.

However, I would add a caveat to scrutinizing my academic record too closely in an attempt to predict the extent of my success at Harvard. From a purely academic and statistical standpoint, my grades are not at the top of the possible range. A linear conclusion from this observation might lead to a prediction that I would do well at Harvard Business School, but would not rank amongst the best or most successful in my class. I feel that this is inaccurate and that a legitimate indicator of my ability to succeed at Harvard would not be based solely on grades, but on what I can add in a case discussion and in a dynamic learning environment. Because of this, Harvard's case method of teaching and learning particularly excites me. I have experienced and learned much in the four years since I left [school]. A case discussion would seemingly provide a forum where success is determined by a display of all of the elements of a worthy education: expressiveness, intelligence and high-quality life and work experiences. I feel that my refusal to limit the measure of my academic success to grades has allowed me to develop these attributes, and that I would do extremely well in Harvard's academic environment.

Comments

The sentiments expressed in this essay are well put. The applicant admits that he can do well at Harvard but that a quick glance at his academic achievements cannot predict all that he has to offer to the classroom experience. He has an eloquent way of stating that he did well in school, he could do better next time, and that he is a well-rounded student with more to offer than strong academics. He never whines about marks that could have been higher. He expresses all cases in a positive manner.

ESSAY 50: Yale, Berkeley, Darden, Duke, explaining a gap

Is there any information not presented elsewhere in the application that might help the Admissions Committee understand your candidacy?

Reviewing my performance and achievements throughout last years the Admissions Committee should take into consideration that for four years neither studies nor career was my most important or time consuming activity. I spent those years taking care of my ill grandmother.

After six days of grandmother's acute condition my mother and I understood, that underpaid personnel of Soviet state health care system could not and did not wish to help seventy-six year old lady. Private medical service was forbidden by Soviet law, so we just took her home. As I knew later, two more days without proper care would have been lethal to her. Taking care of an old lady, who cannot walk, and sometimes even move, is not easy. But I wished to repay my grandmother for all her kindness, her efforts on bringing me up as descent and intelligent person, me as I am now. I was helping her and serving her day and night. I slept in the same room waking up a dozen time every night just to check her. Sometimes it even looked as if we would be able to bring her back into normal, active life. But then illness came back. We prolonged her life by four years and made those years rich and sensible for her. Despite all my professional and social achievements (you can value them differently now, knowing what did it take to reach them) these extra years of life that I gave my grandmother are my main accomplishment of those years.

Comments

The fact that the applicant spent most of her academic years taking care of an ailing grandmother is relevant in the case of lower than average grades. She was wise to include it. She never states regretting the decision—she only states it as a matter of fact. Her poor English obviously didn't hurt her, as she was admitted to the program, but she could have benefited from a grammatical review.

ESSAY 51: Fuqua, engineer, explaining an extra year

What would you like the Admissions Committee to know about you that might not be apparent through the materials in your file before we make a decision?

While pursuing my undergraduate engineering degree, the inflexibility of the engineering curriculum and the inability to seriously pursue extracurricular activities frustrated me. Virginia's Systems Engineering program was rigorous, requiring the most hours for graduation of any undergraduate major and allowing for few non-engineering electives.

My intellectual curiosity and diverse educational interests were not satisfied. I very much enjoyed the engineering coursework, but I wanted more from my educational experience. I had a choice to make: stay with engineering and sacrifice a well-rounded education involving extracurricular activities, or transfer to another program with more flexibility. I chose neither. Instead, I chose to continue in systems engineering but extend my undergraduate education by one year. The extra year allowed me to enroll in a variety of additional courses and also participate in additional extracurricular activities.

The additional coursework, like my interests, included a wide spectrum of topics. Business and economics courses complemented my engineering degree. An English composition course enhanced my writing skills while in the engineering school. A graduate-level Japanese Business and Social Culture course, in which I was one of two non-Asian Studies majors, exposed me to the business culture of an important economic market. I took a European History course because of my interest in the Pre-World War I unification of the German States. These and other courses enriched my educational experience and complemented my traditional engineering coursework.

The additional year also permitted a greater commitment to my extracurricular activities, including serving as a "Big Brother" and holding office in my fraternity. Had I not taken the additional year, I would have continued to volunteer for Habitat for Humanity or Highway Clean-ups. Instead, I committed to spend several hours each week with my "Little Brother", Steve. A gifted middle school student with no father, Steve needed a friend and a reliable male role model willing to make a long-term commitment. I also served as two-term Social Chairman of my college fraternity. While fun, this position also required a significant time commitment, often exceeding 20 hours per week. Both activities were in an integral part of my college experience and contributed to a well-balanced lifestyle. Without the extra year, neither activity would have been possible.

The decision to stay an extra year was not an easy decision. At first, I hesitated because very few students voluntarily choose to stay an extra year in college. I feared that my peers, my professors, and future employers would view my decision as a sign of failure or a lack of motivation. However, the decision felt right. In the end, I was able to continue with my engineering education, enroll in additional courses to broaden my educational perspective, and participate in additional activities to maintain a well-balanced lifestyle. The decision to stay five years counts as one of the critically influential decisions of my life. Looking back, I know I made the right decision. Looking forward, I plan to continue my education with an M.B.A., pursue a professional business career, and eventually, perhaps after retirement from the business community, I hope to pursue a degree in European History and teach high school history.

Application Summary

The relationship between a graduate business school and its students is symbiotic. The school provides an educational, professional, and personal experience designed to provide the skills and experience necessary to be successful in the business world. The incoming students provide a background of diverse professional and personal experiences, attitudes, and skills that enriches the school. Fuqua's educational environment, team-oriented philosophy, and student body combine to provide a unique educational opportunity. I believe the diversity of my professional experience in financial services and my engineering education, coupled with my positive attitude and interpersonal skills, places me in a position to contribute to and thrive in the Fuqua M.B.A. Program. I thank you for your time and your consideration.

Comments

This is a very effective essay. It puts a positive spin on the fact that the applicant took five years to graduate. He has seized the opportunity to explain an issue that might have raised eyebrows otherwise. His decision to stay a fifth year seemed mature, and its ramifications significantly contributed to the rich undergraduate experience that he had. He could have left out the last section, which he entitled "Application Summary."

Reapplication

ESSAY 52: Kellogg, disability, reapplication after rejection

You have been selected as a member of the Admissions Committee. Please provide a brief evaluative assessment of your file.

Mr. John L. Smith, a twenty-five year old caucasian hailing from New York City, is a very dynamic and impressive candidate who would be an ideal member of our entering class.

John's educational background is stellar; while at first glance he may appear to be just another Wharton alumnus, on closer inspection he is truly much more. For one, he graduated from Wharton Cum Laude, certainly no easy task. Even more impressive, however, is that he did so while simultaneously pursuing a master's degree (G.P.A.: 3.6), and he managed to complete both in only four years. His academic majors prove him to be a multi-talented candidate. For his undergraduate major, he selected marketing, while for his graduate degree he chose to study the very quantitative (and obscure) field of Regional Science. This demonstrates he is equally at home with writing as well as regression.

It is obvious that John is very serious about getting the most out of his education. He continues to demonstrate his dedication by applying for the 6Q program, even though he is eligible for the 4Q program. As far as standardized tests are concerned, his G.M.A.T. score of 750 speaks for itself. He is clearly an extremely intelligent and driven individual.

John's work experience is also very strong. He started off like most of his Wharton classmates with a career in banking. However, he soon decided to switch to a profession closer to his heart: marketing. His job appears to be quite demanding; he not only creates sophisticated statistical models, but he also interacts very closely with the finance, operations and administration departments. In order to accomplish all of these tasks, he must have excellent technical, quantitative and interpersonal skills.

His work experience is all the more impressive considering that he was hired in at the same level as recent M.B.A.s. He has obviously performed well, earning a promotion in about a year and a half. His responsibilities also appear to have significantly increased with his new position; he now manages one analyst and supervises another. Come September, he will have benefitted by more than a year of management experience and approximately four years of general work experience.

His career path seems focused. He genuinely enjoys the music industry and is serious about making his future in it. He is also very intent on attending Kellogg. I see here that he applied last year and was denied admission because we felt that he needed more work experience. I believe that his promotion and newly acquired management experience should alleviate those concerns.

John's personal essays are equally striking. In one of his essays last year, he discussed growing up with a childhood illness that left him legally blind. This makes his past accomplishments even more extraordinary in hindsight: they must have been all the more difficult for John, who has limited visual acuity. It is clear from his essays that his experiences as a visually-impaired person have molded John into an extremely strong and mature individual.

Best of all, John seems like a fun and creative person. He's a music lover, an artist and a runner. He strikes me as the kind of guy you'd want on your team, partly for his creative thinking and technical expertise and partly for his ability to kick back and enjoy a beer with you when the work is done.

We should definitely offer John an invitation to join our incoming class. He has repeatedly demonstrated the mental and professional skills required of tomorrow's business leaders along with the character and values that we would be proud to associate with the Kellogg name.

Comments

This essay was a joy to read. Even though it may sound like the applicant is tooting his own horn—that is exactly what he was asked to do. He summarizes his strengths very well and makes a great case for why he should be admitted this time around. He was wise to include a brief note of his achievements since he last applied.

ESSAY 53: Harvard, publishing, reapplication after acceptance

Describe your three most substantial accomplishments, and explain why you view them as such.

Making the decision not to go to Harvard Business School one and a half years ago was the biggest risk I have ever taken. I turned down the opportunity to go to business school in order to move to a new city, look for a job in a completely new industry, and take a 50 percent pay cut. I made such a seemingly crazy move because I have always thought about a career in publishing, and I realized that it was now or never. I wanted to know what I was doing before going back to school: I didn't want to spend two years wondering whether publishing was really the right career for me.

I've made some very large sacrifices this past year in order to pursue this dream. Going out to eat, taking a cab home, buying a new C.D. or even a Coke with lunch, these are all luxuries now, while I once took them for granted. I've had to enter at the bottom of a new profession, which is a lot less glamorous and exciting than my consulting and venture capital experiences. Finally, I had to start over in a completely new field that called on skills I had never before used, instead of continuing to do something where I knew I could succeed.

I knew about these obstacles when I made my decision to go into publishing, but I didn't let my fears and doubts keep me from trying it. And more than anything I have ever done, I am proud of the fact that I had the courage to take this risk in order to do what I wanted.

Second, I am very proud of the work I did at Bessemer. My opinions and the work I did evaluating the deals there played a key role in Bessemer's investment decisions. My enthusiasm for or concern about a particular company affected whether or not the partnership decided to do the deal. The due diligence I did and the questions I raised kept Bessemer from investing in several deals that initially looked very exciting but that turned out to have serious flaws.

I also played an important role in helping one of Bessemer's portfolio companies raise money. Both the partner and I felt a particular concern about the company because it was in a depressed area of Pennsylvania and provided desperately needed manufacturing jobs. The company's C.F.O. had also become the plant manager and was too busy to do any fundraising. So I temporarily filled this role for him, writing the business plan with the investment bank and creating financial projections from the company's model. My work helped the company raise the money it needed to stay alive.

Finally, I have pursued two creative endeavors that have given me a great deal of personal satisfaction—acting and dancing. In high school and college, I was very involved in the theater, playing parts ranging from Desdemona in Othello to the narrator of a children's theater production. Drama has always been a love of mine, and I have enjoyed developing my talents over the years. Since graduation from college, however, the constraints of work have made it difficult for me to continue acting in plays. This past year, I have discovered another outlet for my creativity: ballroom dancing. I spend about three nights each week taking classes and practicing everything from the tango to salsa.

Although both of these accomplishments are purely personal, not professional, I think that is precisely why I am so proud of them. It's a joy to work at a skill for its own sake, whether it's developing a character in a play or working on the proper technique for the waltz. And when somebody compliments me on a part I played or on my dancing, it's a delight to know that I am good at something I enjoy doing so much.

Comments

The applicant utilized this question to reveal interesting (and likeable) things about her. Each achievement was interesting, personal, and commendable. She was wise to explain why she deferred her first acceptance, and her explanation was understandable. Her efforts to save a floundering company in an area that needed jobs were admirable and impressive. Revealing a third achievement that also allowed the committee a peek into her personal life was a smart way to round out an already enjoyable and effective essay.

Accepting Sexuality

ESSAY 54: Kellogg, gay applicant
What is your most valued accomplishment? Why?

My most valued accomplishment is coming to terms with my sexuality. At the end of my sophomore year of college, I was able to admit to myself that I am gay. I consider this a huge achievement, and I value it the most because it was the hardest thing I have ever done and it has had a greater effect on me than anything else in my life.

I say that this was an accomplishment because it would have been very easy for me to ignore my sexuality, even though I knew deep down inside that I was gay. It took a great amount of courage and soul-searching to finally be able to say to myself that I am gay. There is so much pressure from society that encourages gay people to deny their feelings, and overcoming that pressure is monumental, at least for me. Admitting it to myself forced me to re-think my entire future. I had my whole life planned out—a successful career, a family, a house in the suburbs, and so on. My greatest fear was that being gay jeopardized my ability to have a successful career. I believed that by admitting my sexuality, I might have well as destroyed my dream of ever running a large corporation. But I was able to do it anyway, because I knew that this was something too important too ignore.

Being gay is just one small part of who I am, but it has had a profound impact on the way I feel about myself and the way that I look at things. My extensive introspection that occurred when I came out to myself taught me who I am and what I stand for. As a result, I enjoy a sense of confidence that comes from knowing what I value in life. I treasure that confidence in myself, and the clear set of guiding principles which help me make decisions and evaluate my actions. I no longer think that being gay has jeopardized my dreams. To the contrary, I think that accepting myself and gaining comfort with who I am has been a catalyst of my past success, and I know it will enable me to be the future business leader that I have always planned on being.

Comments

The applicant took a risk with this question—not because he discussed his sexuality, but because he chose to do so in the accomplishment question. He may have chosen a more open-ended question as the venue to discuss his pride over accepting who he is and opening up about it publicly. As an essay topic, and an opportunity to reveal his personal side to the admissions committee, it is strong. However, the accomplishment question is utilized by most applicants to showcase achievements that may set them apart from the competition. This applicant could have lost a valuable opportunity by not doing the same.

The Open Sell

ESSAY 55: Chicago, violinist, fraternity volunteer

If there is further information that you believe would be helpful to the admissions committee, please feel free to provide it.

Finding a few hundred unique and qualified people from a mass of thousands of applications is a very difficult task at best. Although I feel that my responses to previous questions provide a great deal of information about who I am and what makes me unique, I feel as though I should describe in more detail two aspects which further set me apart from the crowd. These aspects are my interest and talent for music and my involvement in the development of tomorrow's leaders.

Ever since the fifth grade, I have been very proud of the fact that I have been able to combine academic achievement with a talent for playing the violin. Sacrifices had to be made to find the time for almost ten hours of practice per week, but it has been worth it in the end. During junior high and high school, I was very fortunate to perform with some truly outstanding youth orchestras like my home state's Summer Arts Institute Symphony, my home state's Youth Orchestra, and my home state's All-State Honor Orchestra, in which I achieved the position of Concertmaster my senior year. Solo performances have also been part of my life, both in church services and in competitions for several local awards. Graduate school should provide me with less frequent travel and the opportunity to perform in a local community or university orchestra.

As evidenced by my involvement in my fraternity after graduation from university, I am truly committed to doing my part to help America's youth become better leaders. I have been active both in the local and national levels within my fraternity's organization. At the local level, I have often counseled my chapter's senior leaders on how to run their organization more effectively. I have also advised members at large as fraternity education adviser on issues ranging from effective leadership to ethics. At the national level, I have been an active participant in two of the national conferences of my fraternity. At these conferences I have not only represented my local chapter's interests, but have worked with the national fraternity education committee to improve our national education and development policies and manuals. This summer, I plan to return for a third time to our conference in Chicago and actively participate in the developments of my fraternity.

Comments

Revealing achievements with the violin provided further insight into the interests and capabilities of the applicant. However, his discussion of his fraternity involvement was not descriptive enough and did not significantly enhance his perceived attributes. The essay lacked an effective conclusion.

Part-Time Student

ESSAY 56: Wharton WEMBA, father, part-time student

How do you plan to fit the WEMBA program into your busy schedule over the next two years? What will pose the greatest challenge and how will you deal with it?

It took me a long time to learn that anything worthwhile is difficult. I learned this lesson most directly when I decided to go back to school. What drove me back to school wasn't simply the desire to grow. I made a commitment to myself and I didn't want to take any other path.

During my return to UCLA I was working full-time, had a wife, a 3-year-old daughter and my newborn son. Finding the time to study and do well was quite a challenge. The majority of my classmates were ten years younger and group studying was usually scheduled according to a college lifestyle, rather than one of a professional and family man. I think the question of how I will fit an executive M.B.A. program into my schedule is the same question that I encountered when I went back to UCLA I will fit it into my schedule because I want to succeed. That means that I find the time necessary to concentrate on my schooling.

Discretionary Time

As I have grown, I have discovered that I actually have a large amount of discretionary time. This is the time that I organize to devote to my education. Instead of going to a movie, I study. Instead of driving my car, I take mass transit and I study. I rise an hour earlier and I retire an hour later and I study. I ask my little girl, "How do you eat an elephant" and she answers "bit-by-bit." It took me a long time to figure that out but now I know that to do something big and substantial, I simply chip away at it (bit-by-bit) and eventually I get there.

I picked up some valuable advice when I became a parent. I noticed that I did many things inefficiently. I took much longer to accomplish a task than I could have. Having kids, working, and going to school forced me to identify new ways of tackling my busy schedule. I am now much more organized and accomplish most things in the least amount of time possible.

Being a Parent

Some people say that when you have children you change. As a teenager and as a young adult, I didn't believe it. I believed that when you become a parent, you are still the same person. So it was strange when I held my daughter for the first time. I was in the delivery room with my wife and the moment my daughter was born, they put her in my arms and I felt a physical change. From that moment on, this little girl was my daughter and I would give her everything I could. It wasn't overwhelming or frightening; it was simply a realization—a moment of clarity. I have had other moments of clarity with my kids. When my son was born I felt the same way, and as they grow up, I consistently become more enlightened. The time I spend with my children is the most important time of all, not only for them, but for me. The moments I miss when they are babies are moments that are gone forever, and moments that may shape their lives.

The biggest challenge in taking on any project is balancing time between my family and my self improvement. I handle it by maintaining focus and making every moment count. I always make sure I spend a couple of hours a day with my kids—tuck them into bed, read them stories at night, have breakfast in the morning, and call them when I am not at home. These are the consistent things that keep them feeling loved and keep them on track. This is how I have handled things in the past and how I'll handle them in the future. I will focus on school when it is time for school, focus on work when it is time for work and focus on family when it is time for family. I give my all to whatever I am working on at the moment. For me, that spells success.

Comments

This is a straightforward, endearing essay. The applicant takes a no-nonsense approach to the essay question—he'll manage the program just as he has done in the past. He demonstrates how his ability to balance family, work, and school has worked before and how it will work in the future. His ability to do this, based on his previous experiences, is unquestioned. His discussion of the effect his children have had on him lends a personal touch to the essay and leaves a lasting impression on the reader.

Index